PREFACE

The city has become the residential or gravitational center for virtually every North American. The metropolitan area has become the unit upon which government, business, and the mass media now plan. In short, the rapid shift from rural dominance to an overwhelmingly urban economy and mind-set has taken place within a brief half century. Metropolis is the new form of our society.

For a long time the church ignored the change. Only when her failure to reach increasing numbers of urban people and whole spheres within the city became institutionally threatening did the church rediscover her mission to the city. In some situations the change came too late. For the most part churches continued to operate with a rural model, making only those adaptations demanded by the situation. Within the last decade, however, a growing number of knowledgeable Christians have joyfully entered the urban scene to take part in the task of creating an urban civilization scaled to the full life of man. Their task is not to divert the flow of American life from the main street to the side street where the church building stands. Their task is to move the church, composed of those who consciously call themselves by the name of Jesus Christ, out into the marketplaces of the emerging metropolis. There they meet the world in honest dialog, seeking to convey God's Word as He speaks judgment and grace.

This volume consciously is but an introduction to a complex field of concern. A vast technical literature exists in a dozen subfields of urban studies for those who would pursue them in greater depth. While many volumes exist detailing the work of the church in the city, our focus is on the role of the individual Christian. This book is addressed to him. The urban specialists have conversed with one another for a long time. Contact with thinking members of the church has emphasized the continued gap between the frontiers of the specialist's dream and the realities of church and community as experienced by the thoughtful man in the pew.

In the first two chapters we survey pieces of our emerging urban culture. While indicating the broad outline of urban civilization, we scan illustrative aspects of its problems and challenges. In the next section we look at the change of heart among churchmen which brought them to repentance for past failures in ministering to the whole city. We hope to share some of the excitement felt by those who with abandon have plunged into various ministries within the metropolis. Many have been experimental. Time already is beginning to show deficiencies and to suggest changes. Faithfulness, however, demanded service on frontiers where the roads were not yet clearly marked.

We believe strongly that the process in which we are involved must include two foci: a straightforward look at the reality of the city and a wrestling with its significance before God. While we have kept Biblical references to a minimum, the whole of this survey must be read against the backdrop of God's intention for His creation as revealed in the Bible.

This book is not a practical manual on "church work in the city." We hope that ideas and approaches tried by others might prove stimulating, but no attempt is made to spell out the "how" of programming. Our goal is to begin thinking with you about your role as a concerned Christian in today's city.

The thought and experience of many of God's people, those who humbly claim this title and some who reject it, is involved. Our thanks to them will be expressed most fittingly as you use their insights in further service to God's creatures in the new urban society.

David S. Schuller

CONTENTS

1

MAN AND THE EMERGING URBAN WORLD

Throughout the world mankind is engaged in remaking his habitat. For thousands of years of human history people had to live close to the soil to wrest from it the raw materials for survival. Suddenly in the 20th century this bond was broken. We have virtually reversed the picture. From an earlier day when 98 out of every 100 worked the soil to provide a meager living, now some 7 percent of the American population can produce all of the food and fiber needed for themselves and the remaining 93 percent. The revolution came full cycle when the concern shifted from the number of people who might be released from agriculture for other pursuits to the contemporary question: How many people can our society afford to permit to live on farms?

A Fundamental Shift

One might argue that the situation we face is not new to history, for the story of civilization is the story of people reshaping their world. However, for millennia this change was slow and gradual. The mind-set of simpler cultures was directed to the preservation of their customs and mores. Change was seen as a danger; innovation was viewed as a threat. A basic continuity linked one generation with the next. The centuries passed with relatively little change in the ideas, the arts, or the tools of primitive cultures. Progress was not yet among the chief gods in the human pantheon.

The rate of change now has become so great in the Western world — with the sum result so massive — that our accelerating trend toward a total urban culture poses one of the greatest problems with which we must wrestle as a people. The pace of change is so great that its results suggest that we are dealing not only with quantitative change but also with a change of qualitative proportions. Today the problem of urbanization is greater than a mere series of isolated difficulties. For even if the "urban problems" of traffic, air pollution, congestion, marauding juvenile gangs, racial conflict, adequate governmental representation and control were solved, a *fundamental* urban problem would still exist. We are confronting a change in culture which lies below the level of technology. As a people we are experiencing a change on the level of our values. We can tinker with solutions which seemingly change given pieces of behavior; we can engineer and even gain acceptance of more efficient means of mass transit in our cities; but the basic concern which confronts the man of compassion remains.

The external signs of this massive shift are easily charted. One describes the shift from a pastoral to a manufacturing economy, the line moving from a nomadic existence with flocks and tents to the skyscraper world of our largest cities. One compares the stone-age mallet of 4500 B. C. with the complex computer systems of the space age. From the time of the Neolithic revolution when mankind first began to settle upon the land and engage in primitive agriculture, it has been necessary for the majority of mankind to live on the land. Only a few could be spared rom the basic task of providing food; they served the functions of appeasing the gods, governing, and trading. By definition this meant that only a minority could live in cities. Cities became places of power and prestige. They grew naturally about the functions of trade, religion, and ruling. The court of a local king attracted others who served in specialized tasks, but all were dependent for survival upon those who tilled the soil. The relationship was geographically close and absolutely necessary. Where the hinterland was rich and the climate favorable, a greater number of people could be released from the absolute tasks which made for survival. Civilization is a fruit of this first leisure.

Cities, then, are ancient. The first ones developed with the use of metals — copper and bronze and finally iron. Between 4000 and 3000 B. C. the first cities dawned throughout the Near East. Excavations indicate that the populations of these cities ranged up to 20,000. There was a vast difference between the earlier huts, caves, and tribal tents and the new cities. This represented a revolutionary shift in the manner of living: for the first time mankind was removed from the soil. While individual cities developed and fell, urbanization as a world phenomenon slowly continued to increase. The urban way of life and urban occupations continued to attract numbers of people.

In comparison to a modern city early cities more accurately resembled village life. The lack of adequate communication and transportation severely limited the growth of the cities. Even Athens at its height numbered only between 100,000 and 175,000 in population. Rome alone can lay legitimate claim to being a truly urban center. The best reconstructions suggest a population for the "Eternal City" that varied between half a million to more than a million people. The Romans first developed the unique urban skills of providing for a vast aggregation of people cut off from the soil. Their skills as administrators and rulers made possible the growth of the world's first great city.

The New Metropolis

We shall not chronicle the entire history of the growth of cities, but the conclusion is to be underscored: While cities are of ancient vintage, a truly urbanized culture did not develop until the 20th century. An urban expert summarizes: "For more than a century the world has been moving in the direction of a civilization characterized by the growth of great cities and the pervasive influence of urbanism on human relationships everywhere." Recent history shows that for the first time the majority of humans now live in cities. This urban growth naturally is uneven from one section of the world to another. But it is well for Americans to remember that the two largest cities of the world are in the Orient rather than in the West. Tokyo surpassed New York as the largest city in the world. For a long time the most advanced countries have known a rapidly expanding urban population and a continual shrinking in the number of farmers in the labor force. This will continue to accelerate as a worldwide phenomenon.

In the United States the movement toward urbanization is expanding so rapidly that it stands as one of our most pressing national problems. Unless it can be solved, other significant challenges will become academic. The urban expansion is so explosive that it has made obsolete the very vocabulary we formerly used to describe cities. The old models describing the growth and functions of a city have been strained to the breaking point. We are no longer dealing with the sort of phenomena we knew even one generation ago. To be accurate, we are no longer talking about cities, for the city has become a giant of elephantine proportions. We are speaking of the metropolis as different from the city as the city was different from the village.

Figures serve as an indicator of this change. Fifty years ago there were only three cities in the country which, with their suburbs, numbered a million people. By 1960 there were 24 metropolitan areas in this category. Virtually 90 percent of the current population growth is being absorbed into the circle of land immediately adjacent to our larger cities. The prediction that the end of the century will see over two thirds of our population living in metropolitan areas appears to be too timid an estimate. We continue to move toward the day when two thirds of the entire nation will live in some 19 "strip cities" — areas where population spreads along the highways until urban areas meet. The eastern seaboard was the first to develop what is beginning to resemble one elongated city, extending from Boston through New York to Washington. The remaining 18 strip cities in the process of development will touch virtually every major sector of the country. The urban areas are growing at the expense of the rural community. The rural community is in a process of decline, in total numbers and percentage of the total population and in its percentage in the labor force.

Our emerging urban world can be viewed on a number of levels: We can analyze cities and their role in the history of civilization. We can describe the problems and challenges of the city itself. We can see the difficulties faced by the city resident.

Cities contain amazing similarities. But they also have striking differences. Consider the major northern industrial cities. In spite of differences in topography and types of industries, it is apparent that similar processes and dynamics have directed their growth and produced their form. From a tiny settlement usually located at the point where land and water met, the city grew, adding circle upon circle to its girth. There are the familiar zones of downtown, slum communities, areas of lower-class housing, commercial and industrial regions, and the areas of upper-middle-class residences. Most of the problems of the "inner city" attracting national interest in recent years focus on the varying dislocations that arise in this type of city. The inner cities are a conglomeration of worn-out housing, commercial interests, and residents in great need. These are the cities which have faced serious racial conflicts in the early sixties. The number of unemployed young Negroes and Puerto Ricans has reached volatile proportions. Highly publicized efforts have not erased the realities of ghettoization. The city has had to face the major question of urban renewal while fending off pressure groups and highly vocal individuals on all sides of the issue. The civic and political leadership of such cities is convinced that an adequate tax base would solve all of their problems. But the people of means have moved to the newer rings of the suburbs, depriving the core city of their leadership and their money.

Those who live in such cities as Los Angeles, Atlanta, and Houston find that they cannot correlate their own experience with that described in the reports from the northern industrial cities, for the problems facing the newer cities are of a different dimension. Many southern cities, for example, are still of manageable size. The downtown church still is able to minister to people from the entire metropolitan area. Many of these cities emerged in the period when it was no longer necessary to cluster about a confined center. They spread out early in their development and thus never produced the type of hard-core slum known in New York or Chicago. In oversimplification, theirs is not the problem of decaying inner city; their chief danger lies in uncontrolled urban sprawl. With no authority to plan and provide rational growth and development, the urban area frequently is at the mercy of jostling individual real estate developers and builders. Rich truck-farming areas are invaded by subdivisions. Communities are built without adequate plans for moving additional thousands on traffic-ways already seriously clogged during rush hours. The air is polluted by cars and industries brought into the community. Each segment of government jealously fights off attempts to plan for the broader community. Now that a beginning has been made on some of the worst problems of the older cities, attention is turning to the mounting problems of the newer city.

Meaning for People

Our concern reaches beyond the physical spread of cities and the greater concentration of people in urban areas. We are concerned with cities because of their effect on people. Louis Wirth, one of the first men in America to study the city, defined it in terms of size, density, and heterogeneity. He recognized that when the number of people living in an area moves beyond a certain point, it brings about changes in the relationships of people and in the character of the community. He observed that the greater the number of people who are interacting, the greater the potential differentiation. Similarly, the greater the number of people, the less dependence on any given individual. In the larger community the primary type of contact, as is known within a family, diminishes. Increasingly people meet on the secondary level within defined roles; contacts become more superficial, impersonal, and transitory. The intimate group no longer controls the individual as he moves with anonymity about the city. Because of his association with a large number of groups, the individual knows no allegiance to a single group. Specialization and differentiation are the chief results of the increased density. People and functions are segregated. The city becomes a mosaic of social worlds. Finally, since the city is the result of the migration of peoples of diverse origins, it is characterized by heterogeneity. Without common background and common activities, a new premium is placed on visual recognition. The stranger is judged by make and model of car and by the price and style of his clothes. The larger the city, the less the possibility that one can find agreement on values. There is no common ethical system to sustain the whole community. Inevitably money tends to become the measure of all things for which there are no common standards.

The person suddenly thrust into the midst of the modern metropolis finds that the "traditional wisdom" which he brings from his life in the southern mountains, for example, collapses under the new pressures. His established way of viewing life, dealing with people, falling in love, rearing a family, and earning a living prove to be completely inadequate. He is suddenly confronted with the need for new knowledge, new techniques, and new social modes. That which is true of the poor mountaineer gradually has become true of all of us. We are living in a period that knows a collapse of traditional wisdom. Even more frightening is the collapse of our traditional institutions. It is difficult to modify our ways of doing things, because they are never isolated actions. Our patterns of action are built into our institutions; they are intricately related to one another. But we cannot ignore the failures and near failures of the major institutions of today's culture. The family, the school, the church, the government at all levels, labor unions, many forms of business and industry are having great difficulty in serving as they did in the past. New problems and new knowledge must be integrated with the accumulated wisdom as new demands are made by the culture. When the established institutions fail to meet the basic needs of people, they begin to feel uneasy and anxious; their feelings of alienation are increased.

Regardless of the level of analysis, easy solutions to the problems of the city are impossible. Most of us have a few pet theories to offer as answers to these vexing problems. Where the expert in delinquency, traffic flow, or race is still struggling with the complexity of the problem, the man on the street is sure that given the authority he could have the difficulty eliminated in short order. A solid step toward solution will be taken when we persist in isolating the difficulty and seeing its relationship to the rest of community life.

Urbanization, Industrialization, Bureaucratization

Three fundamental types of pressures come together in the modern city: urbanization, industrialization, and bureaucratization. We have focused on urbanization. Although this is our chief concern in this volume, it must be seen in its relationship to the others. We have said that the increase of size and density involved in urbanization brings about changes in the character of a community; the people's style of life, attitudes, values, and behavior undergo a change. Similarly industrialization involves more than technology and mechanical invention. It involves a radically changed concept of how humans are organized for work. The revolution that took place in the world of industry in the West shows that the principle which developed with Henry Ford was more than a new arrangement of machines and new techniques.

Arrangements of human forces were involved. As Peter Drucker argues, the modern industrial enterprise involves a radically different concept of human organization for work.

When the modern observer compares the worker of an earlier generation with the industrial worker of today, he probably will react first to the lack of skill and lesser creativity on the part of the contemporary worker. While the earlier worker produced the whole product or a substantial part of it, no one in modern industry "makes a product." Each man is restricted to a specific operation. He may have a vague impression of how his job relates to the final complex product; in many cases he does not even "see" his job in the finished item. Further analysis, however, suggests that the modern worker is not less skilled, but certainly he is more highly specialized. This is the first key concept to understanding our modern industrial order. The *pattern* of production occupies the center of the stage; the individual relates to this rather than to a product.

After a given product — a jet aircraft, for example — is designed, the whole must be analyzed and broken down into its component parts; these are further broken down into subassemblies. These then are analyzed into individual operations and the motions of individual machines and workers. But then the opposite process takes place; the whole plane must be assembled from this complex breakdown. This process — integration — is specialization's twin. For a complex item, such as a plane, the preliminary work of analysis, breakdown, and reintegration must be completed before a single plane can be produced. The early stage is theoretical, usually involving scores of tons of blueprints. The time involved may stretch over a year or more. But when the organizational principles are clear, the finished products begin to roll at phenomenal rates of speed.

Modern industrialization indeed affects the former manual worker. Integrating production demands the services of men with high levels of intelligence, imagination, and training. A whole new class of middle-echelon workers — engineers and technicians, supervisors and managers, accountants and statisticians — have been developed to serve this new pattern of production. In all of this we find that people are being affected. Their communities and institutions are being shaped in large part by this process, as former communities were shaped by the work of farming or the demands of the early industrial revolution.

The final step in the process lies in an inevitable increase of bureaucratization. Not only in industry but in commerce and business, in the civic and governmental community, in education and in the church, the total function is broken down into component parts. A large array of manpower becomes essential to the achievement of the goal. We need to remind ourselves that the term "bureaucracy" is not used in any pejorative sense. It connotes a form of rational organization that is in opposition to the informal familistic basis which was known in the past. The church itself forms a useful illustration. Protestantism has experienced the growth of a widespread bureaucracy in the last three decades. Professional managerial types of men increasingly occupy administrative positions in place of former parish pastors who filled such positions during a transitional generation. These new men need objective criteria by which to judge personnel. Pastors begin to feel the conflict between career and calling, as Gibson Winter has pointed out. The new organization of religious activities places a premium on certain skills; men possessing these skills can move with ease from one position to another.

Transformation of Civilization

All of this serves as commentary on the basic fact that a vast transformation of human life is taking place. These factors combine to produce a certain type of attitude that is of concern to the Christian. Someone has referred to the end product as a "technician mentality." It is composed of a mental outlook which is positive that it can solve all problems. It is the attitude of the man on the street who expresses confidence that eventually anything can be done. "We'll find a way" is his expression of faith and hope. Implicit in this attitude is an emotional attachment to progress. Progress is an unquestiontioned good in life. As a matter of fact, failure to progress appears to involve sin. A thoughtful examination of this mentality shows further that it restricts its concerns to immediate goals; the ultimate ends are rarely questioned. Because of the size and complexity of modern life, we see a system which has been set in motion. Dealing with immediate goals, we may have a sense of fulfillment and finality. No one, however, fully perceives where the total enterprise is going.

A final characteristic is an increasing focus on human manipulation. Generations ago our forefathers turned their energies against raw nature; our energies are turned toward the manipulation of one another. This is not entirely negative. We have greater knowledge today about commnity change and the unconscious motivations of people. The community *can* use this knowledge in a constructive fashion. But we tread the thin ice of taking God's place and reducing people to objects.

In an essay Jean Ladrière discusses the dangers of the technician mentality. It makes for a concentration of power and human decision. With more instruments of power in our hands than ever before, more human decisions about their use must be made. In everything from the use of insecticides to the atomic bomb we are faced with decisions that will affect vast numbers of people—and finally our world itself. Furthermore, as techniques are improved as a means of dominating nature, man quickly becomes another segment of nature to be controlled. He is emptied of much of his meaning as man. The result is the disappearance of the sacred. Concentration on technique often obscures the question of significance. As Norbert Wiener, the founder of cybernetics, once said, "We have learned to answer the question *how,* but we are no longer capable of answering the question *why.*" In the place of meaning we are left with technique. The world is desacralized; mystery disappears; the possibility of a transcendant God lessens. The world appears transparent. The gulf between the Scripural frame of reference and that of the modern day increases to the breaking point.

A Christian Perspective

It is a rich picture: one of light and darkness, of exploitation and service, of despair and hope. An entire city follows the rescue attempts to free a small girl who has fallen into an excavation. Yet the same city cheers when thousands of people are burned alive in an atomic explosion. But beneath the surface of life familiar to all, the Christian sees another dimension. He views the city and modern culture with added insight. For he understands sin; he knows that it is more than ignorance or the occasional slip from the noble. He knows that many utopian plans are destined for tragic failure because they have not acknowledged the demonic forces of evil in our world. The Christian views the world in the light of the Redemption. For in spite of sin, God has loved His creation. His Son became one of us to rescue us from the evil of which we are always a part. We see the world under His rule and lordship. It takes the eyes of faith to make this affirmation. But we do affirm this because by His life, death, and resurrection a new age has broken into time. Though evil and death are real, they are doomed by the greater reality of His presence and power. This is the Biblical meaning of hope. This is not a Pollyanna desire that everything eventually will work out satisfactorily. It is the confidence that because once Easter followed Good Friday, God's will and purpose will be done on earth — in spite of all the evil struggling against His will.

The Christian therefore enters the world with a sense of responsibility and joy. His concern is not to escape into a warm corner away from pain and suffering. Discipleship calls him to enter the world as Christ entered it.

This involves a number of steps, concerned Christians have discovered. First we must learn more about our urban culture by entering into its life. We must face the world as it is, not as we would ideally reconstruct it. A responsible Christian cannot be an escapist. Then comes the moment of theological reflection. In the light of God's revelation regarding Himself and man, society and the church, creation and the sacraments, we ponder this reality. This step is more than a translation of agrarian concepts into urban equivalents. It is the moment of pondering God's will for our day — with the resources provided by God Himself.

Those at work in the most difficult situations of ministry insist that there is a necessary third step: worship. They call it the "cement" which holds together the first two. Here a person comes close to God — in study but also in prayer and praise. This is the moment of receiving God's own strength in the Sacrament and celebrating Christ's presence in His world. Only the man who is engaged in life is able to come to worship with expectancy. He comes thirsting and questing; he comes *from* life in order to return *to* life. But the process is not one of using God but of being used by Him. We face the reality of the urban world and the reality of God's will for mankind in an urbanized culture. God speaks both judgment and grace. He would bring His message through His people.

22

2

HUMAN PROBLEMS OF THE URBAN WORLD

Problems cannot be dealt with in the abstract. We cannot concentrate primarily on incidence rates showing the ratio of cases per 1,000 population. We need the ability to fix two points in our vision at the same time. Our focus must be on the specific case of need; otherwise we fall prey to the technician mentality. But to avoid superficiality and sentimentality, perspective is needed to put each problem of need into its place on the broader canvas.

Within One Family

It is possible to see many points of need within a single family in the city. Consider the actual case of a family of six living in the slum area of a large midwestern city. The antiquated dark building which houses their living quarters is in a state of serious disrepair. The hall has a pervasive odor of human bodies, tobacco, cheap whiskey, and decaying wood. Upon entering the family's apartment you see at a glance all of their possessions. A large metal bed dominates the room; the blankets remain as they fell when the last person arose. A single bare bulb provides the only illumination for the room. A table and two chairs occupy the center of the room. Leftover food is on the table, along with dirty dishes. A number of tin cans serve as ashtrays; several are full and overflowing. To the people there, this is "home."

The father is not an old man chronologically, but he is dying of sclerosis of the liver. His heavy drinking has taken its toll. His story is a simple one. His formal education ended with the sixth grade. When he was in good health he supported himself and his family by retrieving golf balls from the water traps in the plush golf courses between Texas and Missouri. The teen-age son has dropped out of school and is following in his father's vocational footsteps. The mother completed the third grade. She apparently loves her children but has few skills to serve them capably. She too has begun to drink more heavily. The family's only income in recent years is from various welfare agencies.

Two children are playing on the floor. They pay no attention to the old, second-hand TV that blares away in the background. An older girl is in the fourth grade. Will the school and the Sunday school in which she has recently enrolled be able to help her and her family break the cycle that even now is dictating the direction in which the next generation must plod? The child smiles and scrapes the scab on her soiled knee.

There is no hostility here against the rest of society. Instead tired, apathetic acceptance of the whole situation prevails. Life is lived hour by hour.

Its Implications

If this family pulls from us nothing more than sympathy, we miss the most important point regarding the city and its problems. For the problem is of greater magnitude than simply an isolated case of poverty or the effects of limited education or excessive drinking. We do not remove responsibility from the individual when we insist that attitudes and behavior patterns are the products of social experience. A youngster from a privileged home may reject the gifts bestowed on him and slowly destroy himself. But the child growing up in the home just described has never received the fundamental skills necessary to compete in modern America. The ignorance, the illness, the lack of basic hygiene, the mismanagement, the failure to see one's self and purpose in life—all of these will permanently stunt the lives of the children who develop in this setting. These are not smug middle-class judgments upon modes of life at variance with those to which we are accustomed. We are facing realistically the skills necessary for economic and social survival in our society.

The man of compassion who would help must look below the surface where the manifestations of immediate need in this family broaden out to touch many of the major institutions of our day. On this level we investigate the whole economic picture and ask about employment possibilities for men with limited productive and personal skills. We look at the educational system which failed to truly engage these parents while they were youngsters. We ask about the community agencies which failed to impart fundamental concepts of personal hygiene and house-keeping. We inquire about the conditions which permit housing situations of this type to exist—not only on the part of the owner of the building but also the city inspectors who have not reported violations. We speculate about the church which has made tenuous contact with the family through one of the youngsters. Has it played a significant role in the community in the past? Will it be able to touch the lives of this family in a meaningful way?

The picture is clear. The roots of the problem reach into many sectors of the community. Help directed to the surface needs of the family is inadequate. Moreover, it becomes harmful if thereby the more fundamental issues are not faced by the community. In the immediate future churches or service agencies may serve by setting up remedial reading centers for children from disadvantaged homes and schools. But the responsible agencies must be made to face their assigned tasks of providing an education for all children entrusted to their care.

The problems, then, of the city are the concerns of groups as well as individuals. And the first step toward solution or partial amelioration demands the patience to seek the cause of the difficulty as well as its more obvious manifestations.

The problems of the city today are myriad. Whole volumes are devoted to single aspects of urban difficulties. A vast technical literature has developed on air pollution and the movement of traffic. When we reach the level below the purely technological questions and explore education, politics, and employment, virtually the whole of American culture comes into our purview. Here we shall focus on six areas as illustrative of the major problems to be faced constructively.

Interracial, Ethnic, and Religious Tensions

When the Supreme Court issued its momentous decision outlawing school segregation in May 1954, the question of race as manifested in segregation ranked as the most serious domestic issue facing the United States. As thousands of pages of testimony in the hearing mounted higher and higher, the nation loudly proclaimed its conviction that the racial issue was more than an economic, political, and social one. The churches, through spokesmen on various levels, insisted that we were dealing with a matter which had a strong moral and religious core. Until that was faced by every institution and person in the country, we would deal with only a shadow of the real problem.

Critics arose to ask that the churches evaluate their witness and work for understanding and justice. Martin Luther King, Jr., spoke bluntly:

> *Honesty impels us to admit that religious bodies in America have not been faithful to their prophetic mission in the question of racial justice. In the midst of a nation ripe with racial animosity, the church too often has been content to mouth pious irrelevancies and sanctimonious trivialities.*

While men of goodwill were agreed on the ultimate goal, there was violent disagreement regarding the methods to be used to achieve the goals. The battle began between those working for racial equality and those resisting it. Three basic approaches were taken. The first group insisted on orderly procedures. They made use of the courtroom, worked to have new laws passed, and used the mass media to persuade people. At the other extreme were those who exercised violence. Sections of many cities were shambles after clashes by angry mobs. Bombings, beatings, and murders were the means used by this group. Most significant, both theoretically and from the viewpoint of permanent change, was a new order of politics that stood between the two extremes. It was termed "nonviolence." But it represented a different mentality from those who worked strictly within the existing legal situation. Its techniques soon became familiar. The sit-in in all of its forms, mass demonstrations and marches, economic boycotts, school boycotts, and rent strikes made daily news. The public was confused by this approach; Christians were quickly divided. The majority

27

preferred less active means of pursuing racial justice. But a small minority, heavily represented by the clergy, joined in the demonstrations.

Admitting it as an oversimplification, one student of the racial struggle, Arthur Waskow, described the different philosophies underlying the three approaches to change. In the approach of orderly politics, men follow the rules. In the approach of violence, they attack their enemies. In the approach of nonviolence, they pursue change. Whether or not one agrees with the analysis, he must admit that more change has been effected by the third method than through either of the first two.

At first many people in the South felt threatened as the rest of the nation attempted to solve the "southern race problem." It soon became apparent that this was not a sectional difficulty. While the problem assumed a different form, the difficulties posed by racial and ethnic differences in northern cities were equally severe. Residential segregation often is more rigid in the North than in the South. In most cities a relatively small proportion of the total city blocks contain the major part of the entire population of the minority group. The pattern is even more striking when one compares the number of Negroes living in the older section of the city with the number living in the newer and better communities of the suburbs. In St. Louis, for example, approximately 30 percent of the city is Negro; only 3 percent of the population of suburban St. Louis County is Negro. About 4 of every 10 homes occupied by Negroes in that city were classified as substandard in the 1960 census. The local Urban League further estimated that at least 70 percent of all Negro homes were located either in slum or blighted residential areas. Many cities were shocked to discover that, in spite of a decade plus of efforts through slum clearance and urban renewal, the Negro housing situation in the early sixties was relatively as bad as it was 10 years earlier.

Obviously the Christian must respond with more than personal goodwill. These complex problems will not disappear simply because he is a social liberal who recognizes members of minority groups as fellow human beings. To help in an urban world, he must take the additional step of action. To be effective, this usually will involve action in concert with other people. Since residential segregation is the basis for many other forms of segregation and injustice, the Christian might begin here. A number of cities have groups actively seeking to achieve better understanding between peoples of different races. Some arrange for introductory visits between two couples of different races. It is surprising how many people have never visited with people of another race with similar interests and background. Other groups are active in their neighborhood, attempting to prepare the ground for the day when a Negro family may desire to buy a home there.

Housing and Urban Renewal

One of the most crucial and perplexing problems of the city lies in its facilities for housing people. Not only does housing consume more land than other functions of the city, but it also becomes the key to other difficulties, such as traffic congestion, the relation of the central city to the suburbs, etc.

If priority is determined by extent of need, our greatest concern remains with those who live in delapidated, substandard housing. The data of the 1960 census were shocking. Despite the great wealth of the United States, one sixth of our urban population—representing over five million families—lived in slums. This means that the buildings were overcrowded and/or the areas extremely undesirable. A full eighth of our urban population live in dwellings that are in poor condition or lack sanitary facilities. Most of these people lack the necessary income to move to more adequate housing. Particularly since the Housing Act of 1949, the Federal Government has appropriated large sums of money to demolish slum housing and provide low-cost public housing for these families. Some progress was made in the first decade of this program. Many critics, however, question the extent to which the 1949 legislation aided. The major problem occurs on the local level when the city receives the financial aid. Cities currently appear to be less concerned with providing housing for the disadvantaged. They are wrestling with ways of achieving adequate tax bases to provide for the welfare services which such families demand. Thus many cities are demolishing slums with funds originally designated for housing—but the cleared land is used for business and industry. An analysis of the 600 projects involved in urban renewal at the close of 1962 found that while almost all of the areas were residential prior to clearance, only some 350 would be residential when rebuilt. To further magnify the problem, many of the residential sites were designed for middle- and upper-class housing.

Slums stand as a monument to a greater love of property than of persons. Sensitive Christians have asked how such conditions come to exist and to be perpetuated. If they investigate, they find that some of the "slum lords" are hardened individuals who have found a way to make a "fast buck." The average person fails to see how one can get rich by taking money from the poor. The returns on slum properties can be unbelievably large. By breaking an old single-family dwelling into 8 or 10 apartments, the original investment can be paid for in a few years. By doing as little as possible by way of maintenance, the slum lord makes three to four times as much on his investment as would be possible through any other means. Some owners of slum properties, however, are kindly people who are regular churchgoers. They have invested money with an agent who handles all the business matters pertaining to the building involved. The owners often do not care to know where their property is. They enjoy their earnings more fully if they are not forced to see the misery behind their profits.

The larger community has endeavored to regulate this condition. Most cities have ordinances that make housing conditions of this type illegal. But it remains difficult to provide effective inspection and conviction with penalties severe enough so that they would not be viewed only as a recurring nuisance by the slum owner. As indicated, urban renewal was designed to attack some of the worst conditions. It is easy to become partisan and to describe urban renewal as the program which will change dreams into reality, transforming ugly hard-core slums into garden apartments. But it is equally easy to focus on the mistakes, suggest political involvements, describe the hardship of the families who lost their homes, and, above all, to highlight the confusion resulting from the red tape involved in dealing with dozens of federal agencies.

Thus we have another instance where the man with Christian sensitivity is needed. Most would agree that the task of providing housing for the low-income third of the nation cannot be made appealing to investors; thus if it is to be done, heavy government subsidy will be required. There are several groups in the average community with strong vested interests in the outcome of decisions regarding urban renewal. Along with the many technical decisions to be made, there are the decisions involving people—ultimately the whole community. Those who participate in the decision making must be informed of the financial, political, educational, and civic aspects of the question. At the heart of these significant decisions lie moral and religious questions that seriously concern the world which God created. Above all, they concern people whom He created and whom He loves—even when they have little political voice.

Amos spoke some of his sharpest denunciations to religious people who withdrew into their homes of luxury, eating fine foods and enjoying themselves while the poor were trampled. God still despises our religious assemblies when they do not result in letting "justice roll down like waters, and righteousness like an ever-flowing stream." (Amos 5:24)

Employment

Cities develop primarily because of the jobs they offer. The current urban revolution in work is undermining the city by rapid withdrawal of former job opportunities. We have awakened to the fact that our labor supply no longer fits the shape of the new demand for labor. Even during the period of President Kennedy's administration the cybernation revolution had reached the point where he called automation the major domestic challenge of the sixties.

The inevitable dislocations have led to major employment controversies. Industries automate in order to remain competitive and to increase profits. Unions fight to safeguard the jobs of present workers. The greater questions relating to people, poverty, and racial injustices rarely are raised. In spite of those who argue that there is no technological unemployment, we face a situation where many men are dismissed from jobs that will be performed by machines. Displacement is an inevitable part of the process of automation. Both industry and government have tried to ease the burden on the individual. For some, displacement means unemployment. For others it means securing a new job—at times the same type of work in a new place. More frequently it means retraining for another task—usually one requiring more skill.

It is significant that this shift is so basic that it affects the unskilled worker at the bottom of the economic scale and will increasingly affect middle-level management. When one airline company installed a giant computer in its reservations system, more than 50 junior executives were displaced. Even highly skilled people in decision-making positions will be replaced by computers capable of making decisions on certain levels more precisely and more accurately than human beings. Men in this category usually find other positions without undue hardship.

Those who suffer most are people with few skills to sell. Unemployment is identified increasingly as a problem of the unskilled worker, the worker with obsolescent skills, the young worker, the Negro, and the older worker. These categories obviously represent a large segment of the American working population. Openings for professional and technical personnel will continue to absorb a great part of the total work force, but openings for the young man with the skills and dispositions to hold only low-paid routine jobs are shrinking rapidly. Automation means that the overall skill level of employment has pushed upwards.

A serious situation becomes even more serious when we relate automation to the problem of race. When white immigrants came to industrial cities several generations ago, industry welcomed them. There was need for their physical power. Through hard work they were able to provide an adequate living for their families. But as the new immigrants come to the cities today from the backward mountain regions or the poor rural areas of the South, industry no longer needs them. The civil rights revolution is taking place at a time when the Negro-come-of-age is no longer needed in the lower-skill jobs.

The experts in automation are concerned that many informed people fail to grasp the magnitude of the industrial change that has occurred. Economist Robert Theobald emphasizes the basic difference between the former industrial order and the new socioeconomic order. During the indus-

33

trial age production was based on a combination of man-power and brainpower. In the age of cybernation manpower is practically eliminated. Theobald believes that economic problems emerge from the complete inability of the present industrial system to deal with cybernation. One shares the concerns of Richard Bellman of the Rand Corporation, who indicated a conviction of many experts that "in the discernible future" 2 percent of the population at "the upper administrative levels will be able to produce all the goods and services to feed, clothe, and run our society, with the aid of machines."

But the problem is more than economic, technological, and sociological. We must ask about human values. God designed man so that he needs more than goods. He needs the concomitants of work: purpose, a sense of accomplishment, a way to serve others. His very position in society is determined largely by what he does. God gave the command to work in Paradise, prior to the fall into sin. The use of leisure becomes a challenge to our society. Freedom from back-breaking and deadening types of jobs can be either blessing or curse. The emerging problem lies at both extremes: supplying jobs for those with deficient skills and providing meaningful quality to the increased free time of those who hold jobs.

Education

The problems of education in the large city are manifold; perhaps the most pressing one is a more adequate education for the disadvantaged child. What can the schools do for the youngsters described earlier? We are dealing with a large number of children. Studies in the mid-sixties indicated that 40 to 50 million people make up the most seriously deprived group in the nation. The proportion of children affected continues to increase in the large cities. "In 1950," Frank Riessman tells us, "approximately one child out of every ten

34

in the fourteen largest cities of the United States was 'culturally deprived.' By 1960 this figure had risen to one in three . . . By 1970 it is estimated there may be one deprived child for every two enrolled in schools in these large cities."

The schools as presently constituted have great difficulties in reaching these children. Teachers and administrators often see them primarily in terms of problems—discipline, truancy, carelessness in work, and finally dropouts. The culture which these children represent is not compatible with that of the schools and the dominant culture of the country. The schools presuppose a family background that will bring a child to a certain physical and emotional level prior to his entrance into the school system. It further needs the home to support its program by providing the child with aspiration, social skills, and help in achieving. The disadvantaged home, in contrast, is more frequently characterized by poverty, instability, a lack of discipline, and, above all, an indifferent or hostile attitude toward formal education. Thus at every point the culture of the home and the street fails to prepare the child for school. Beginning with the basic ability to use the language and to read, the child is expected to have skills and attitudes which he has had little opportunity to develop at home. Thus, from the beginning, the experience of school often is one of discouragement and deepening pessimism until the day when he drops out of the system in which he has always been an alien.

The picture is no longer all black. Several experimental projects conducted in the largest cities of the United States have made great strides in identifying points at which change can be made to aid such children. These programs utilize major adaptations in curriculum, organization, instructional materials, and equipment. Other programs attempt to raise the child's level of aspiration by exposing him to elements of culture in the city which the average slum child has not met. Many areas utilize the period prior to entrance into kindergarten to compensate for some of the child's deficiencies. Remarkable changes have been effected. This is clearly a problem to be met by concerned groups other than only the school and the individual home. The community itself has a big stake in the outcome of the battle against ignorance. American cities are paying more for the effects of poor education — welfare, delinquency, and crime — than they pay for education. There is no single key to unlock all of the problems that lie on the two sides of this difficult situation — modifications in the existing school system and in the attitudes of the children themselves. But it is another area in which the concerned Christian and the congregation can perform an honest service to people.

Local Democracy

The average middle-class American who lists the major problems of our cities probably would not include this item. For him democracy is a safe and shining ideal to be taken for granted in his community. The sad fact is, however, that a sizable part of our urban dwellers are politically voiceless. These are the faceless people at the bottom of the socio-economic scale. Other groups in the community control the power and make the decisions. While there is a conflict of interests between strong unions and large companies or between two political parties, it is among these groups that we ultimately discover the power to make decisions within the community. At the bottom are the people and the subcommunities who have no spokesmen. They receive little of the service which every citizen is supposedly entitled to. When problems arise and they suffer exploitation, there is no one to represent them.

Community organizations have sprung up by the scores throughout America to fill this need. Violent controversy, charges and countercharges swirl about their very existence, to say nothing of some of their goals and tactics. Community organization is an attempt to organize members of a community for the purpose of improving their own locale. Ideally their interests should include various aspects of the community—education, health, housing, employment, city planning, social welfare. Their efforts should not be restricted to one sphere. The goal is to work genuinely with the people. The most controversial figure in this field, Saul Alinsky, insists that those involved in organization work need to work directly with people—not *for* them or *over* them but *with* them. Great stress is laid on grass-roots participation.

This appears sound and very safe. But the rub comes at two points. First, to achieve their goals usually means direct conflict with the interests of the group already in power. No group gives up power without a struggle. Alinsky and others scoff at the type of organization that is a philanthropic plaything or the kindly gesture of a group toward social service. He is involved in nothing less than a bare struggle for political power. Alinsky argues that the only reason for banding together is to create an instrument for power: "The power concept must be seen nakedly, without the sordid raiments which serve more as disguises for our own inability or unwillingness or timidity to get involved in a controversy in which we may get smeared or hurt." He feels that controversy is inevitable when a group of "have-nots" band together against the existing institutions within the community for the purpose of making specific demands. Those whose approach emphasizes education and conciliation more than does Alinsky's would argue that they do not seek the ascendancy of a new segment of the community over another. Rather they seek a new and better balance of democratic forces. Their goal is a renewal of community spirit where all of the people work together for the good of the whole community. In each approach the church has a vital contribution to offer. Where the church is not seeking selfish goals it can serve as an agency to promote justice in the community.

The second conflict arises from two radically different schools of thought regarding community development. The first group frankly builds on self-interest; the second group attempts to work with a sense of altruism. Similarly there is a difference in the degree to which conflict or reconciliation is used. The first group utilizes raw coercive power; the second prefers education and persuasive negotiation as the means for social change. Finally, the first group works for a partisan identification of the members who have banded together; the others seek an identification with all parties in the conflict.

It is apparent that in this instance something is needed beyond the well intentioned do-gooder. Christian groups are at present widely separated in their support or rejection of the Alinsky approach. Some see it as utilizing methods which utterly reject a Christian understanding of life and community; they feel that sinful methods are used to accomplish a good end. They question his autocratic methods and his insistence on conflict. Others support this approach, feeling that it is not as crass as it appears and that it stands as the only method which may effect social change. Increasingly the areas to which we are called as Christians no longer appear in clear blacks and whites. We are in the midst of moral ambiguities. And it is precisely here that we must struggle; it is here that we are most needed. Here the word of judgment and grace needs to be spoken; here the church can truly penetrate the world. As Christians participate in local community organization they will come to know the issues, the resources, and the real leadership in the community. They will be able to bear witness to the Christian ethic in the issues under debate. The church thereby will be able to participate in policy decisions that will affect the future quality of its community.

Traffic, Air, and Water Pollution

There are other great needs in our emerging urban culture. The city dweller is familiar with many of these as the more crass liabilities of living in an urban area. Urban planners still are not agreed on how to handle the ever-increasing number of cars on city streets and expressways. Between 1940 and 1955 the number of cars in the country doubled; predictions are that another doubling will take place by 1976. The projected figure of some 113 million vehicles will produce an urban paralysis even more severe than the present one. Motor vehicles also demand an inordinate amount of space for roads and parking. For example, two thirds of the entire downtown area of Los Angeles is devoted to garages, parking lots, and streets. For decades planners have realized that the ultimate solution cannot lie with current plans of increasing expressways. For by definition expressways generate more traffic and thereby produce a worse situation. Most agree that a fast, clean, and dependable system of rapid transit provides the only long-range answer.

Automobiles are the principal cause of air pollution. In the Los Angeles basin some 80 percent of the air pollution was caused by automobile exhaust. Areas which have never experienced smog are plagued with the problem when the number of cars and trucks in the area increases. In many cities (Birmingham, Ala., is a prime illustration) air pollution has become so bad that through normal breathing one may be taking in as great a quantity of cancer-causing substances as would result from smoking two packs of cigarettes a day. From the outset of the factory system in England, this problem has been faced by cities throughout the world. Humans, animals, and plant life are seriously affected by our pollution of the very air we need for life.

Growing cities are polluting the water supply of America. Rivers and streams carry human sewage and factory discharge from every community upstream. With sickening realism the publisher of the St. Louis *Globe-Democrat* told readers: "Every time you take a glass of water from a faucet in St. Louis, you are drinking from every flush toilet from here to Minnesota." Unfortunately this is true across the country. In many communities the amount of detergents in the drinking water is so great that it foams as it comes from the faucet. In the brief period between 1955 and 1961 city sewer systems were dumping twice as much waste into rivers and streams as was considered allowable in 1955. Over 50 million pounds of solid wastes are pouring *daily* into our waterways. Someone described our cities' water as thin soup of dead bacteria floating in a chlorine solution. Furthermore, as our urban populations continue to increase, cities will be forced to bring clean water from ever greater distances. Los Angeles soon will be piping its water from as far as 550 miles away.

Christian Reflection

Many of these problems appear to be purely physical and thus remote from Christian concerns. But they must be of concern to the Christian. It cannot be overlooked that the most significant criticisms of modern urban conditions have come from those concerned primarily with the physical welfare of the community. Too frequently their efforts have remained on this level. Most Christians approach the areas of urban need as neophytes. They may be experts in professional fields dealing with the city. But as a group conservative Christians have given little serious attention to asking how the witness of the Christian faith relates to the problems of life—body and spirit.

Some general guidelines will help our thinking. First, the urgent problems associated with urbanization are becoming worldwide. The World Health Organization's report in 1964 indicated that the degree of urban expansion throughout the world is growing at such a pace that it has become an international problem on a par with the question of nuclear war. This is true of countries on both sides of the Iron Curtain.

Second, the Christian is concerned with all of God's creation. Our commitment to Him as Creator involves a concern and a trustee relationship to all of the created world. Therefore we must be concerned about the pollution of water and air as well as with the unnecessary destruction of valuable farmland in the uncontrolled sprawl of suburban developments.

Third, the Christian's concern for people extends to all areas of life, both physical and spiritual. We are involved in where they live and how their children are educated, in their opportunity for employment, and in presenting the gift of Jesus Christ. We are concerned about the distribution of welfare aid as well as with rat control, and as much concerned about what goes on in the world as with what goes on in the church.

Fourth, a resolve to begin work must be made in spite of the complexity of the situation and the paralyzed feeling the individual experiences as he weighs his potential contribution against the ocean of need.

Fifth, Christians are not alone in their concern and in their willingness to work. Churches are not the only institutions that have a stake in these issues. Because Christians will be working with others of different motivation and background, they will need the understanding, the encouragement, the correction, and the sustaining of a group of fellow Christians to insure a distinctively Christian contribution. In a day when decisions are influenced ever more heavily by groups and organizations, Christians must learn to deploy their forces singly and in groups.

Two phrases that recur in the collects of the church embrace these thoughts. Frequently we pray: "Stir up, we beseech Thee, O Lord, the will of Thy faithful people . . . that we may serve Thee in willing obedience." God must touch our hearts that we might become sensitive to needs which assume a different face in our day. We beseech Him to grant us the vision and the courage to be obedient in an emerging urban world.

God's Word still speaks to our day. In Micah God developed one of the great champions of the poor in the Old Testament. Micah's spirit burned with righteous indignation when he saw people being oppressed. He knew the immorality and corruption of his day, the hatred among classes, the rejection of God's voice, the desire for wealth and power at any cost. But Micah had absolute confidence that God's purposes would triumph, for God would send the Divine Conqueror, whose victories would not be by might or by power but by His Spirit. As post-Easter Christians we celebrate the victory of this Anointed One, our Lord Jesus Christ. We now seek to fulfill God's words given through Micah: "He has showed you, O man, what is good; and what does the Lord require of you but to do justice, and to love kindness, and to walk humbly with your God?" (Micah 6:8)

3

REPENTANCE: OUR FAILURE IN CHRISTIAN WITNESS

The morning paper in a small southern city carried the story. A young Negro man had shot someone. In reporting it as a human interest story, the newspaperman tried to reconstruct the Negro's background. What had brought him to that moment? In the middle of the story stood the pathetic picture of the church. The young man had gone to Sunday school and church in a larger city at a Negro mission started by white people. It stood as a showplace to indicate to suburban churches their concern for all people. Repeatedly as a child he was lined up with others when visitors came to demonstrate how even such young-sters as he could learn hymns and recite Bible passages. When white visitors asked what he was going to be when he grew up, he learned that the favored response was "a minister." Church people read the story. Some felt betrayed after all they had done. Others were disturbed, questioning once again what the church really was doing.

The church cannot blame itself as an institution each time a person gets into trouble. But it *is* forced to reevaluate the effectiveness of its work. Many of her methods are being examined to determine whether they still are valid responses to the faith in our new urban world.

Disturbed Christians

The last decade has seen a lengthening line of men within the church questioning the goals and methods of American churches in the latter half of the 20th century. They describe the church as an institution that has made peace with the surrounding culture. Instead of a courageous and prophetic witness, they hear nothing beyond a pious echo of the basic values of the culture. Instead of initiating action, the church appears to be a major agent in preserving the status quo. It is domesticated. It continues to sing heroic hymns about the sons of God going forth to war, of marching in the noble army of martyrs to meet the tyrant's brandished steel, of climbing through peril, toil and pain — but all tacitly understand that the hymns are to "inspire" and are not to be taken literally.

It began as a small cloud on the horizon. Criticism of the churches, sharper and louder, began in the early fifties. This stood in sharp contrast to the forties, during the years of the war, when criticism of churches and clergymen was entirely absent. It was of great significance that the most vocal and precise criticism of the institutional church came from within the churches themselves. Specifically, theological thinkers and sociologists joined to force the church to look closely at herself in the mid-20th century and to redefine her functions and goals. The names of the major prophets became household words, at least in the household of the church's leadership — Herberg, Marty, Berger, Winter, and Stringfellow.

The criticism came when the churches were at the very height of their success. They had reached more people organizationally than ever in their history. Over 65 percent of the population held church membership. Budgets doubled, and then doubled again. Religious publishers were turning out more material — and of a higher quality — than ever before. Church construction zoomed. Using 1947 as a base year, the value of construction in the early sixties reached 500 percent. The indebtedness of people to construct these buildings had soared to more than 700 percent. Churches were crowded. Programs were successful.

Success or Perversion?

But then the quiet voices began to ask whether the church had won the world but lost its own soul. Churchmen wondered if they were involved in the most colossal perversion of the true church since the days of Constantine. It became increasingly difficult to be certain of the continuity between the church described in the New Testament and the form of church life known in the average congregation in America. Clergymen began to look at their buildings and programs with a jaundiced eye. Were the congregations, in many cases, the local country club at worship? Were they class churches — voluntary societies of like-moneyed, like-colored people who subtly or not so subtly set membership requirements that related more closely to one's position in society than to one's discipleship? Were the large, old-line denominations fleeing their responsibility in the older areas of the city where peoples of other ethnic and racial groups were moving in? Were they selfishly reestablishing church buildings and establishing new congregations in the name of "mission," when actually it was for the greater convenience of settled church members and those whom they might lure from other city churches? Were they spending most of their time and energies in keeping the ecclesiastical machinery running and paid for? Had their means and ends become so completely reversed?

But the criticism didn't stop there. In 1955 Will Herberg wrote that Protestantism faces "what has so far proved an insurmountable challenge, the urbanized, industrialized America of today." Churches were under attack for continuing to live with a nostalgia for rural America while the society had become urbanized. Closely related to this issue was Protestantism's traditional individualism. The critics suggested that this excessive individualism owed more to the philosophies of the Enlightenment than to the Bible. An editorial in *Christianity and Crisis* called for theological reconstruction:

> *Contemporary urbanized society has made that individualism obsolescent. Power today is socialized by giant corporations, labor unions, and governmental agencies. Protestant personalism has a valid protest to make against the "organization man," but the protest cannot be made effectively by invoking a futile individualism. The need is for a reinterpretation of the relation of man and society—a task of theological reconstruction for the church at large, not merely for its theologians.*

The reconstruction must focus on the question of the audience to which the church would address itself. Most churches have restricted their proclamation to the personal difficulties of the individual. They speak to the problems of doubt, guilt, and death. No one who knows the Biblical record can deny that these problems have Biblical validity. But the question confronting us is whether faithful witness and service to the unique situation of the 20th century will not demand a witness to the broader spheres of life. Most congregational preaching and teaching aids the individual as he faces life personally, in the circle of his family, and in face-to-face relationships. Virtually no thought or aid is given to the Christian as he makes decisions in business and commerce, in government and foreign affairs, in medicine and higher education. A realistic appraisal of the role of these institutions demands that we see them as more than the sum total of their individual participants. This means, then, that God's word of judgment and grace must be proclaimed not only to individuals but also to the structures and institutions of our society.

Life in our increasingly urbanized culture is not an integrated whole as it was in the rural past. A serious division has occurred between the community in which man lives and the one in which he works. In the residential community we have the complex of sleeping, leisure time, household chores, and worship. At some distance geographically is the community in which modern man works, has his business contacts, and spends the major portion of his daylight hours. For most men the latter community is the most significant area, the one given priority and the one that counts most in their thinking.

The Residential Trap

This comes to the heart of the question of responsibility. In the culture that is developing, should the church be associated so exclusively with the residential? Should it deliberately seek to associate itself with the sphere that has become the area of leisure? The residential area is characterized by family life, peopled during the workday by women and preschool children. Certainly the emphasis of every main-line denomination reflects this preoccupation of the church with children and individual counseling problems. In addition, the "community" about which the local congregation is concerned is its "own" community. This means the immediate residential area in which it is located. Are we perpetuating an outmoded form? In the rural past there was a *single* community, and the church was a part of it. Now there are two communities—the private residential community and the public community of business, commerce, government, and higher education. It was not by design but by historical development that the church became trapped in the first sphere.

The most serious consequence is that the voice of the church means less and less in the arenas where the major decisions of life are being made. Big decisions in the industrial world, the world of government, and in the world of education are made on an entirely secular basis. This is to say, they are being made without reference to God. The individuals making the decision may be pious men who acknowledge the existence of God. But for the most part the church has failed to address itself to the public sphere where the man functions, and thus it does not adequately understand his role in corporate decision making.

The church has taken two alternatives, both of which appear to be inadequate. On the one hand the church has encouraged each man to "be a Christian" on the job. In the complexity of the modern business world, however, he regularly faces decisions and policies which he feels conflict with his personal ethical standards of consideration, forgiveness, a second chance, honesty, and integrity. Thus he reduces this responsibility to a personal plane that has nothing to do with the large decisions being made. The other option—equally untenable—is to suggest that when a man fills a specific calling, he must abide by the rules of that game and perhaps carry out decisions which would conflict with his beliefs as a Christian.

The responsible church must witness not only to the personal but also to the *public* sphere in the 20th century. It must witness to groups and institutions as well as to individuals. We are forced to reexamine some of our most cherished clichés: "Religion is a personal affair." "The church must not get into politics." "The church should keep to its own sphere and not become involved with the secular sphere." Each cliché contains a germ of truth; each is deadly to an effective witness to the 20th century. The Christian faith is personal, but the Christian has social and public responsibilities. If "politics" involves the arena where decisions are to be made, can we say that this is an area where the judgment of God must be excluded? Is there a safe "spiritual" sphere in which the witness and work of the church should be isolated?

Private vs. Public

To summarize the challenge: In an expanding industrialized, urbanized culture we are experiencing a bifurcation of the public and the private sphere. The church is associated almost exclusively with the private sphere. Consequently more decisions of greater significance are made on the basis of financial, military, social, productive, and medical considerations than on the basis of religious and ethical considerations. The church unconsciously augments the "secularizing" of our culture when she encourages private piety apart from public responsibility. We do not suggest the opposite error — so complete a focus on the public sphere that the private sphere becomes paganized. Currently we are in urgent need of a reappraisal of the manner in which our men, money, and physical resources are deployed. In the average city, how much of our energy and concern is addressed beyond the pale of the private sphere? The question of social responsibility is not a pleasant "extra" for the church in an affluent age; it lies at the heart of the question of how the contemporary church can bring a witness to Jesus Christ to people living and working in this society.

The form of the challenge is new; the call to obedience is constant. God's people were called to this responsibility during Biblical days. No one can read the prophets without an awareness of their demand for social justice. Amos,

Hosea, Micah, and Isaiah are often referred to as "the ethical prophets" of the 8th century B. C. Our Lord's own ministry is a singular commentary upon the compassionate service which He directed toward people. The early church as depicted in the Book of Acts demonstrated a quality of service in caring for those in need which proved that faith flows immediately into acts of concern.

But the Holy Scriptures are never interested in ethics or ideals in themselves. Biblical ethics arise from the worship of God. Notice how the Ten Commandments were given. They begin with the reminder that people are to act in a particular way because of God and His mercy. The Commandments are prefaced: "And God spoke all these words, saying, 'I am the Lord your God, who brought you out of the land of Egypt, out of the house of bondage.'" (Ex. 20:1, 2)

A man who walks in covenant with God walks to a different drumbeat than does the man of this world. Furthermore, the Commandments and the general thrust of Biblical teaching regarding responsibility are very specific. They are addressed concretely to persons and particular communities of people. Biblical thought does not deal with general principles or abstract ideals. Justice for Biblical writers is not a Platonic concept; it is embodied in specific decisions and actions made by men over against other men. Further, we need to recover the Biblical sense of urgency. In the Biblical material there is an imperative tone that we are in danger of losing. In answer to the question of the great commandment in the Law, Jesus replied with the imperative: "You shall love the Lord your God with all your heart. . . . You shall love your neighbor as yourself." (Matt. 22:37-39)

But some would still disagree. They would insist on a purely individualistic interpretation of the Christian faith. The pattern of congregational life that was possible and necessary in the rural past remains normative and prescriptive for them. As the churches entered the "world" in the early sixties and became involved with the issues of race and poverty and scores of other questions on which churchmen felt it necessary to speak, some laymen drew back in horror. Clergymen were told rather bluntly to "keep their noses out" of issues that didn't affect them. In some street demonstrations angry mobs told the pastors to get back into the church "where they belonged." The more sophisticated suggested that they were well intentioned but somewhat sentimental. They should stick to their particular areas of competency and leave the world to businessmen and politicians. Faith indeed had been so completely isolated from expression in life that its reappearance was met with fear and violence. Most shocking of all, some were convinced that such expressions of an active faith must be communist inspired!

Theological Rediscovery

Two fundamental needs are highlighted. First, the church must deepen her own awareness of herself as "the people of God." Christians must rediscover a sense of discipleship that strikes deeper than external church membership. In Biblical usage the term *people* connoted a greater unity than does its English equivalent. Every person was seen as being set into various relationships — a certain people, nation, and tribe. The "people" to which an individual belonged told a great deal about him. Thus to say today that a person belongs to the "people of God" should describe many crucial factors about him.

Too many people use clergymen as their representative "holy men." Clergymen are expected to personify spiritual traits; a laymen is expected to sin. The clergyman sometimes becomes the last backstop to prevent the layman's falling into complete godlessness. Even active churchmen express the fear that if they were to conduct their business according to the principles propounded from the pulpit, they would be bankrupt within a month. In each phase of their public sphere, then, a subtle discounting takes place. They shade the ideal in the light of practical business experience. But the moment of truth must come for the laymen. *They* are the church. *They* are the *people of God*. The pastor is *not* a professional holy man who lives a righteous life in their behalf, but a man to whom God has given gifts to be used to support and strengthen the faith life of people. Again, the Gospel is able to enter most situations only as it is borne by Christian men and women. Pastors are to aid a man in growing to a certain level of spiritual maturity and understanding. But the man himself is the one who lives the life of faith in in his various roles.

Second, we must be sensitive to areas where the witness of the *entire* Christian community is necessary. In the rural past a single local church, if it was strong, could influence a community. The present generation is conscious of the conflicting voices resounding from a dozen churches located on a dozen different corners, representing a dozen different brands of Christianity. Churches are now struggling to witness effectively in a period when Protestantism no longer is the assumed background of the majority within the community. Or even where it is, a greater concern for the religious sensitivities of others has forced the group to reconsider what formerly was a rather autocratic approach.

Excessive Congregationalism

It is strange indeed that congregationalism—the relative freedom given to the local congregation—has become a major obstacle to the exercise of serious social responsibility in many areas. To be effective in the type of society we now know, it is necessary to plan many endeavors in cooperation with other churches and agencies. The decision to begin a new mission in a particular subdivision must be made in the light of needs elsewhere, availability of other churches to serve the area, the decisions of other groups to build churches there, availability of pastors, etc. This demands cooperative planning. "Congregational autonomy" has become a sacred cow which occasionally turns into an idol that disrupts what appears to be the wisest course the churches could choose. Pride, tradition, stubbornness, and a genuine desire to work become so intermingled that it is difficult to evaluate the motivations of the church that prefers to "go it alone." Sociologists who have looked objectively at the crisis situation in the inner city, for example, have bluntly said that excessive congregationalism will continue to kill off urban churches. In their judgment only churches with episcopal forms of government — and thus some overall direction and control — will be able to weather the storm of the inner city.

We are not advocating a monarchical episcopacy — the use of bishops in whom rests the power of decision. Numerous illustrations from other areas of the world indicate that social problems are equally serious under bishops. Our plea, however, is that we move beyond our present inability to meet problems where necessary on a higher level of authority because of a view that restricts the operation of the church to the local congregation. We begin where we are. Some cities are striving to meet this need through strengthened councils of churches. Some churches are reorganizing so that the jurisdictional unit which corresponds to a metropolitan area is strengthened. We need the fundamental mind-set among Christians that refuses to permit necessary witness and service to go undone because of the resulting demands upon the local congregation. Necessary coordination begins as each congregation evaluates its program in the light of unique community needs and the resources and strengths of neighboring churches.

We must repent. We have loved our comfort more than we have loved God. We have depended on our traditions more than we have trusted Him. We have loved our churches and organizations to the point of idolatry. We have spoken of humility while pride of accomplishment swells within our breast. Loudly we have proclaimed our arduous work for God, but in the witching hour we wondered whether we were exerting ourselves for our own glory. The witness of the church at many points has become little more than a weak echo of the basic beliefs and attitudes of the world. True, the terminology is more pious, but too often we reflect the unbaptized world. We need to repent, but we stop short. "The face of complacency is seemingly intensified by the way in which men beat their breasts and at the same time continue to function along traditional lines," observed George Webber. "Flagellation takes the place of repentance." To repent is not a sign of disgrace or impotence. It is the first step toward healing.

When we repent, we "come clean" concerning the source of our problems. We will cease pretending that a new program or gimmick will change the basic conditions of our churches. The fifties probably will go down in the annals of church history as the decade of "the project." Mass programs of every variety were promulgated by the agency bureaucracies within the denominations, councils, and local churches. Self-studies, spiritual life missions, preaching missions, stewardship programs, mission projects, educational training programs — each promised to be the panacea to revitalize the local church. The machinery continues to grind away in the mid-sixties — though with noticeably more skepticism and less enthusiasm than a decade before. Our basic needs continue to be theological and spiritual. We must see ourselves and our churches under God's judgment and grace. We must move back into the Word to see our condition. We need God's help to effect more than just another temporary adjustment of the ecclesiastical mechanism—and thus miss another opportunity for honest change.

Jesus Christ claims lordship over our lives. This makes us servants—an extremely difficult relationship for us in modern America to grasp. In our new role as servants we will be released from the bondages which now wear us down. We devote much of our energy in life to proving our worth. We pour out our lives in an effort to find meaning in life by ascending above our neighbor. And then from the lonely heights our basic alienation haunts us and we seek unity once more. This double pattern lies behind most of our anxieties and frenzied actions.

In His life and death Jesus Christ freed us from this futility. He uncovered our sin—so deep and frightening that comparisons with others become meaningless. Still He loves us. He grants us a worth and meaning before which our petty strivings become the play of children. He comes to us in spite of our exaggerated pride. And He binds us to Himself and to our brother. The reality is there when a person refuses to acknowledge it or even actively denies it. Worship, then, takes on meaning. No longer a sterile exercise, it now becomes the setting for joyful participation with brothers. The Word is received as food. The Eucharist is a thanksgiving—we proclaim the Lord's death with joy! Within the body of Christ we need God's reminder that our First step is repentance, not an attempt to right ourselves with Him. We repent—repent of our fear, our hatred, our self-love, our disobedience. And the miracle is that God causes new life to grow out of this very sin and deprivation.

4

NEW VISION AND NEW BEGINNINGS

Repentance leads to new beginnings. A prayerful consideration of much of the organizational life of our churches has
forced us to see it for what it is. Membership drives are
a poor substitute for mission efforts. Hat shows sponsored
by women's guilds are no more sanctified than those held
under secular auspices. Men spend long hours in church
basements making decisions that affect little more than the
household chores of the church. Poor teaching in church
classes cannot be excused because of the nobility of their
original purpose or the piety of the teachers. Collective
selfishness on the part of a church is no less a sin than is
personal selfishness.

Christians are beginning to understand that we are living in the midst of a great bending period of history when
change occurs so rapidly that fundamental change is de-

manded on the part of all institutions in the culture. The Gospel does not change. But Christians find themselves examining each part of their corporate life that in time has become inviolate to change. A new era of history is opening. Faithfulness to our Lord demands the best offerings of our minds and hearts as we seek ways to proclaim the Gospel and to offer ministry to a new world. We must take history seriously. Our Lord entered into time; we, His servants, live in time. It forms the stage on which we live and serve.

Early attempts to update programs and to introduce projects stirred temporary interest, but the fundamental issue remained unresolved. We tried to "come clean" with ourselves. Initially we thought the problem was simply one of antiquated church organization. But it lay deeper than church structure or polity. New programs, new constitutions, and new curricular materials made people uneasy; when they failed to effect the desired change, despair deepened. It became apparent that we were dealing with a problem of deeper dimension than we had realized. It dawned on us that we were attempting to put patches of various sizes on old wineskins . . . but we feared giving up the old skins. So revolutionary were the changes about us, however, that effective response demanded more than a slight adjustment of the mechanism. Slowly we became less defensive and less fearful. We asked what we were striving to do in our world through the Gospel. We looked at the rising new world and humbly sought ways to proclaim the Gospel.

The Incarnation

People were moved by various ideas in Scripture. Some emphasized that the church as the body of Christ must serve as the extension and perpetuation of Christ's incarnation. Just as Christ entered human life and knelt

57

down in the midst of suffering humanity, so His body today must assume this stance of compassion and service. Christ lived a life in close dependence on His Father. At the same time it was a life that was wholly open to men. Within Jesus' life we see the perfect fulfillment of His own summary of the Law. He loved the Father with total heart, mind, soul, and strength; and He loved other men as Himself. His life was characterized by the Gospel writers in a term difficult to translate into English. At best we can say He "had mercy" or "compassion." But the word implies a great intensity and depth in the giving of one's self. He so entered into the situation of the other—into his sin, pain, and lostness—that the other's suffering penetrated into the center of His own being. The despised, the outcast, the sick, and the rejected sensed this concern and were drawn to Him.

Moreover, in Christ, we discover the pulsating rhythm of life—a withdrawal for prayer and refreshment, and then renewed and intensive service. Prior to the crucial points in His ministry, we find Jesus spending long hours in prayer. Strengthened by communion with the Father, He pours out His entire life in compassionate service. Finally, as we view the sweep of His entire ministry, we see His reaction to the changing moods of the people. During the early part of His ministry the crowds flocked about Him and accorded Him warm admiration. But a break came, and the popular gatherings ended. Only a faithful few continued with Him. Prior to His crucifixion even the disciples deserted Him. But His work and attitude did not depend on popular approval. As the dislike of the crowd intensified, His own love and concern for them increased.

Many within the church now find in our Lord's life incentives for their work and models for their responses to the Gospel. These characteristics—a total focus on the Father matched by "compassion" for people, the alternating rhythm of withdrawal for prayer and return to service, love that ministers faithfully in spite of a lack of popular support and even open hostility — provide significant guidelines for His body today as we seek to minister to our newly emerging world.

Lutherans usually have begun with the concept of the church or of the Word in their attempt to fashion a response to the Gospel in the modern world. Their view of the church normally begins with the local congregation. The church is present where people gather about Word and Sacrament. They grant the fact that many churches have not been creative and innovative in actively seeking new avenues through which to proclaim the Gospel to those for whom the organized church is an alien institution. They fear that some Protestants have sought bridges to the culture, only to find that after the bridge of communication and understanding has been established they have no real message to proclaim. In this dialog, then, they bring a needed emphasis on the Word of God.

Church and World

Another group of Christian thinkers has helped in reviewing the relationship of the church to the secular world. Historically the church has fluctuated in its relationship to the world. In periods when the world seemed extremely corrupt and evil, the church adopted the monastic reaction of withdrawal. Others have sought active contact with the world of thought and culture by attempting to present the Gospel in as favorable a light as possible to the thoughtful skeptics. Those who call the church to a "true secularity" are conscious of the pitfalls that lie on each side. But they also are convinced that a paralyzed refusal to act is not the answer. These men struggle with words through which to best convey this thought. They are attempting to distinguish a "true secularity" or a "holy worldliness" to which God calls us from a spurious secularism, an unthinking accommodation to the beliefs and actions of the world.

This group affirms that God sends His people as knowledgeable saints to open frontiers in areas of the world that claim exemption from the Word of God. They frankly stand in opposition to the brand of churchmanship composed of good, safe, conservative, "religious" people who remain safely isolated from contact with a sinful world. They seek to take seriously the lordship of Christ over all of life — not only the life of the church but of all creation and of all institutions. Many are shocked to hear these men say that we must act out realistically the message that Jesus Christ is not only Lord of the church but also Lord of General Motors and the Democratic Party. The Creator will not be restricted to a small human sphere which we define as religion. The rest of life cannot thus escape the will of God. The call to a true secularity is a call to a faithful witness to the world which God created. It sees the individual as part of a much broader culture. Its heart is witness and not morality. This is no attempt to "Christianize" the social order. For the Scriptures see the heart of evil in the demonic rather than in ignorance, social environment, or poor personal adjustment. The Christian today must beware of the trap of pessimism which condones irresponsibility before all of the decisions that must be made in social life.

Driven by the God who has sent them into the world to witness and to serve, conscious of the failure of some of the older forms through which these tasks were carried out, aware of the world which claims autonomy from God, Christians have sought new avenues through which to work in our world. We shall examine some of these under three larger categories. Some of this renewal is occurring within existing parish structures. Other significant work is taking place within groups of parishes. A third type of ministry is being carried on outside of the parish structure.

In areas where the urban change has been most intense, the former rural patterns of operation within churches have been under the greatest strain. The rural pattern presupposed stable family units, relative residential permanence, a favorable Protestant disposition, some knowledge of what the church is, common work patterns within the community, and a scarcity of other community agencies. Churches in the inner city have found a situation that is a complete reverse of the rural and village pattern. The basic outlook and the specific patterns that so ably served the rural situation failed to make contact with the true urbanite. As former members moved away and older members died, the established churches began to face a dark day. Memberships tumbled rapidly. Many congregations that once numbered 1,500 to 2,000 members experienced decline down to 100 or 200 members. The organizations dissolved as leaders moved away and morale dropped. A discouraged little knot of people gathered on Sundays in churches built to seat 10 times their present numbers. Some finally merged with others in equally desperate straits. A few closed their doors altogether. Others moved to the suburban areas where many of their former members had retreated.

Another group, however, stopped and surveyed the situation. A look at their communities disclosed that in many cases they contained more people than when the church originally was built. They saw human need. And they remembered that God had sent them into the world to make disciples of the nations, baptizing and teaching. They had not gone to the world, but God obviously had moved the world to them. With vision and trepidation, often with more commitment than knowledge, they chose to remain and serve the people who lived near their church.

Perhaps the most dramatic step that a church of this type

takes is to make the initial decision that it will become a church to all people in the community—regardless of racial and ethnic differences, family background or social standing, moral standards or police records, whether working or lifelong recipients of relief. For a church that has been a tightly knit, homogeneous group, representing primarily one type of national background, perhaps even conducting some worship services in the original mother tongue, such a change evidences the work of the Spirit. This is the initial hurdle. But it is one that a group faces repeatedly—when the goodwill of the congregation is tested by vandalism, when attacks are made on people in the community while involved in church service, or when the realization dawns that little fruit is harvested in proportion to the fantastic efforts expended.

The church then responds to the needs about it. A congregation finds that youngsters in the community are handicapped all of their lives because of poor reading ability. Perhaps half of the teachers in the local school fail to meet the minimum requirements set for teachers. Churches have responded by opening reading clinics and providing tutors to work with youngsters after school. The church may merely initiate the program and then recruit workers from every available source. Another church finds that juvenile gangs have taken over some of the roles vacated by families. But the gangs are becoming destructive. The rumbles and intergang fights lead to stabbings and thus arrests by the police. Some churches have stepped in to provide the gang a place to meet. They are not going to make altar boys out of most gang members. But an understanding Christian who has lived through gang life in his own youth is able to reach out to them as fellow human beings, with no ulterior motives. A few pastors with great patience have established a relationship of trust with one or two local gangs.

Such areas are in desperate need of counseling services. Some churches have arranged for a team of men—perhaps three drawn from psychology, psychiatry, law, medicine, and social work—who come to the church one evening a week to meet those seeking help. The ones who come have been encouraged by others who have been helped. The church has made prior contact with the local hospital, mental health clinic, family counseling service, pharmacists, special training schools, and the like. Since the average person in the lower strata of our society either is suspicious of such groups or totally unaware of their existence, the church provides the immediate service of listening to their problems and indicating where help is available. When no other agency is equipped to help, the church utilizes its resources to provide the needed service. Churches quickly learn that it would be poor stewardship to try to set up a parallel set of structures on their own denominational level. But the church is needed most desperately where it is closest to people and in the cases where no existing agency can provide the help.

Many aged people live in rooming houses and older apartments in these areas. Some are alone, with no relatives in the city. No one cares about them. Some churches have responded to this need. Their basic philosophy is not to serve these people and make them dependent on the church, but to provide the opportunity and the channels through which they will be able to serve one another. Some furnish a gathering place where senior citizen groups can organize their own activities in the fashion that will serve them best. Others arrange for those who are physically well and able to move about the city to meet those confined to their homes. Thus friendship and needed services are given and received.

The congregation that moves closer to its community soon asks if it must wait for tragedy to strike before it can help. It seeks preventive measures in place of remedial work. When the crime rate among Negro youngsters is five times that of white children, the need is deeper than simply dealing with each youngster *after* he gets into trouble. Churches find themselves fighting on the side of their people who face the exploitation of the established community. Social education is needed to acquaint people with their rights. Social organization is needed to provide the vehicle for presenting their just demands to the broader community.

Interparish Ministry

It is evident that, when dealing with the problems of the modern city to which the Christian must address himself, the problems are too big and too complex to be handled by a single congregation or even by a particular denomination. We have many examples of several congregations within a given community banding together to accomplish certain tasks in common even while each congregation continues with its own parish program. The North Side Cooperative Ministry in Chicago, for example, is an organization of some 24 churches and two settlement houses. These churches represent seven different denominations. While each congregation carries on most facets of its former ministry, areas of service previously neglected now are addressed through the strength of joint effort. Some of the work carried on by such groups is similar to that already described. They direct their efforts toward youth, education, and the elderly. Group cooperation can undertake work that would strain the resources of a single congregation. For example, the entire field of arts and the church should serve the broader community; it can well draw upon the greater Christian community for participation and support. One church has drawn to itself a group of people who are interested in drama. At regular intervals they present illustrations of the newer drama through which playwrights present the plight of modern man, and some of the work of noted Christian dramatists who are wrestling both with man's dilemma and God's redemptive action. The broader Christian community can better sponsor community-directed services. One group provides clinical services, augmenting the badly overtaxed hospital. Another provides for lectures on hygiene, baby care, and housekeeping for women whose formal education is deficient and who are new to the ways of the city. Churches have engaged Spanish-speaking pastors where there is a large Mexican or Puerto Rican community. Still others provide classes in English.

These problems weigh on the hearts of all Christians. Unfortunately our modern city makes many of the most pressing problems invisible to the Christian who lives away from the center of town. The two worlds no longer meet as a car speeds through a depressed area on a modern expressway. Many middle-class Christians have not responded because they are unaware of the problem or of ways in which they could be of concrete help. Some imaginative Christians devised the idea of matching an inner-city congregation having specific needs with a suburban congregation that needs to avoid the smug isolation which can close in so quickly. An inner-city church was eager to sponsor a vacation Bible school for its community but lacked the necessary personnel, organizational skills, and financial resources. A suburban church joined hands with them, and together they sponsored the school. In other cases the need was for physical aid in working on a classroom or sponsoring a basketball team or teaming up with local members for a religious canvass of the neighborhood. The danger is that the deepest needs of the inner-city community will not be met if those from the outside come with preconceived goals and plans. The needs of the two communities differ greatly. Where a false type of religious colonialism can be avoided, these programs have been helpful to both the giving and receiving congregations.

Even these changes, however, failed to penetrate that important segment of our world which we refer to as the public sphere. As Donald Benedict concluded, ". . . it appears impossible from the geographical parish base for men to respond to the central issues of public policy or to penetrate the corporate structures of the world of work." In the past we recognized, at least to a limited degree, the necessity for work beyond the parish. Chaplaincies to the military, to hospitals, and to colleges have a relatively long history. To meet emerging needs, this concept must be radically expanded. For example, many perceptive Christian leaders sensed the irrelevance of the church to the center of our industrial society. Men like Episcopalian Bishop Richard Emrich observed that our society is dominated by great corporations, but the church is ministering only to families, and "the world of work becomes a lost province." Therefore a group in Detroit began the Detroit Industrial Mission. Its goal was to meet with men in industry, management as well as hourly production workers, over the moral issues they face in their jobs. Meeting during lunch breaks and shift changes, the groups discuss the bread and butter of their own concerns. But as the DIM staff believes, every major decision that men make involves a moral question. To the question, "Where does religion fit in?" one of the clergymen in the group quickly retorts, "Where is it missing?"

There is also a need to work with executives and businessmen. Some churches are concerned about releasing a pastor from a residential parish to cultivate a "downtown ministry." His parish is not limited to a geographical area. His ministry is to the segment of society that works in the downtown area. His presence stands as a parable of the concern of the church for all areas of life and as a symbol of Christ's lordship over all of life. Practically, he begins by establishing a relationship of trust with the businessmen he meets. It takes them some time to believe that he is there for a purpose other than getting them to join a church or to contribute to some cause. For those who sit high on the management hierarchy, who fear opening up to subordinates regarding some of the deeper issues of life that plague them, and for the most sensitive on the lower rungs, these men stand as pastors.

Perhaps the coffeehouses stand at the opposite end of the scale. In a number of cities groups of Christians have opened coffeehouses. They offer them as "free ground" where the church can meet in open discussion with those who because of hostility, reasoned belief, or indifference would never enter a church. The coffeehouses are usually basement rooms done in a style that reflects the artistic, informal attitude of those whom the church seeks to engage. Their goal is not proselyting or membership gain. They intend to form the setting for dialog — a place where the church can listen to those who may feel a great hostility toward the middle-class world that the church seemingly represents. It is a place where Christians can join the conversation about some of the "gut issues" of life that many young people are concerned about. The actual program varies. One evening may present a reading of a drama or poetry. Perhaps a folk singer provides a musical background for a half dozen discussions going on in various parts of the room. Often a local painter will have a display of his works on the walls.

Another significant experiment in "taking the church to the streets" is the series of Faith in Life dialogs conducted in several midwestern cities. This is an American adaptation of the *Kirchenwochen* in Germany. The key is dialog, which provides the setting where people can talk with others about the problems of daily life and their faith. Taking seriously the structures of society, the church tries to provide men who will be able to enter existing structures with credentials that will gain them acceptance in their own right. These people go, however, conscious of themselves as part of the people of God. They take part in the regular gatherings of the community. Service clubs, movie houses, waiting rooms in hospitals, places where farmers gather, the city hall, cafes and restaurants become places where members of the team—laymen and clergy alike—go to talk. By design their task is to begin dialog—not just to talk and analyze but to listen. Special gatherings with doctors, youth, the aged, parents, public officials, and pastors are held. In some cities the mass media are the major vehicle for meeting the community. Endeavors are planned as useful means for demonstrating to an entire community the church's concern for the public realm. They also show concretely an area of mission where Christians of various denominational backgrounds can unite to work at their central task.

Between these categories is the growing trend to establish "house churches." In a public housing project, for example, a church may discover that thousands of people are not served by any church. But they quickly learn that the conventional approach of stable churches does not touch the residents. In contrast, the pastors have carried out significant ministries by gathering small groups of residents in a series of apartment meetings. Some gather about the study of Scripture. Others discuss specific problems of their life—rearing children in project areas, the safety of their building, the responsibility one has to other families, how a family can get along without a father, or how to handle a teen-ager who is about to drop out of school.

In a similar category is the new movement of churches into community life, displaying a greater sense of responsibility. In a given eastern city the question of *de facto* school segregation was a major issue. The community was torn into two rival factions. The first inclination of a local church was to avoid the issue and neutrally serve both sides. But it became apparent to the leadership of the church that some definite moral issues were involved. The church therefore could not remain in the background and avoid the issue. It commissioned two members to seek out the facts and present them to the church council. The congregation was eager to provide its members with the necessary background to evaluate the alternatives from a Christian perspective, in addition to the social, economic, and educational values involved.

"The church must look for new vessels for its message and explore new forms of ministry and witness if it is to be alive again in the inner city." This is the conviction of a group of Christians who have banded together for more effective service in Chicago. It states the belief of every Christian who would serve the emerging urban world with joy.

5

ACTION – NOT TALK

Many of the men ministering in the inner city give the impression of being "angry young men." Their desire to minister is strong. But it is matched by their admitted inadequate knowledge of the situation, by limited resources, and by middle-class backing that often seems to freeze the status quo. They realize that, instead of remedying basic causes, they exhaust their resources in simply handling the next crisis. Their frustration builds up. The people whom they are trying to help remain apathetic or angry, ignorant and fearful. The helping agencies appear beset with slow-moving procedures, incompetence, and the desire to remain safe.

A young man spent a summer working in the inner-city area of Indianapolis. When autumn came, he did not return to Yale. As the months wore on, his frustrations increased.

Speaking of beating his head against the twin brick walls of the ignorance and inertia of slum people and the lazy or pompous personnel at the city agencies, he wrote in a letter:

> . . . *I come to think more and more that anything short of either a massive federal program of people dedicated and sensitive (which government programs seldom attract) and money, money, money, or a bloody class revolution that will make race riots look like Geneva peace conferences (something that if it is going to come may not be too far away but will probably never come), will never solve anything.*
>
> *If people were genuinely, honestly, and openly concerned about the situation, there would be some hope, but very few are. We have scores of middle-class churchgoers who come from the suburbs saying they want to help. I'm afraid the only thing they really want to help is their conscience. They'll give parties for the kids and the old folks; they'll help with kids' groups at the Center, but when we really get down to the center and begin trying to do something about slum landlordism, inadequate hospitalization, and the non-existent realistic treatment of alcoholics, bribed health inspectors, housing programs, etc.—when we really get down and it becomes evident that the poor are poor because the rich are rich, when it becomes evident that the establishment is so firmly entrenched under the banner of the Puritan ethic that a man should work for what he gets . . . then our fine middle-class helpers begin to chant Wait, Wait, Wait, young man . . . and we find that $5,000 has been withdrawn by the contributors because they didn't want us to do anything about the causes of poverty; they just wanted us to run a community center and church and maintain the status quo.*

The indictment is clear. As Christians most of us will go along with minor adjustments in our personal style of life and in our society that seem to be more humane and alleviate some of the world's need. But when it becomes evident that the change must be primary enough to disturb our own comfort, we quickly lose interest. There have been few fundamental changes in our society, because as Christians we have only talked about them. We have not worked for them. We lack a basic commitment strong enough to drive us to action.

Commitment

Douglas Hyde sensed this failure of Christian leadership. Hyde is a former communist who was news editor of the London *Daily Worker* before his conversion to Catholicism in 1948. Hyde has endeavored to stimulate among Christians the same conviction and ability to act that he found among communists. He has observed that converts are drawn to the Communist Party by the idealism, dedication, and willingness to sacrifice shown by its members. At the beginning they rarely know anything about communist philosophy. They are drawn into a campaign; there they begin to associate with communists. In these people they come to see men and women of fantastic dedication. Hyde tells of the young lady who rose before dawn each day and pedaled a bicycle to a London railway depot to sell newspapers to arriving commuters. Or the 200 newspaper workers at the *Daily Worker* who wanted to do more than edit and produce the paper. They finally accepted the suggestion that they all volunteer to give blood. Their plan was to continue to return time after time until they established trust and friendships, and finally converts. All 200 volunteered. One worker donated so much blood that he collapsed. Why? Because each communist worker believes he lives in a decisive period of human history. He believes he is fighting something evil and corrupt. He is willing to perform heroic acts because he is fighting in a great global battle. Every day and every action is important.

This attitude represents the spirit of the church in the days of her youth. But this is not to be a lament for bygone days. For the Spirit who invigorated the church of the first century remains the One who strengthens and empowers today. In some ways our problem is compounded. We no longer hear the Word with pristine freshness. We have learned to discount the words, to adjust the radical demands, to change the wild, joyous promises and demands of the New Testament into a call to middle-class piety. But when Jesus promised the presence of the Spirit, He said He would be with us forever: "The world cannot receive Him, because the world neither sees nor knows Him; but you know Him, because He dwells with you and is in you. I will not leave you bereft; I am coming back to you" (John 14:17, 18 NEB). The Spirit still wants to fan the glowing coals into blazing flame.

And so we need more than good intention. In spite of goodwill, we are often allied with the forces that exploit the very people for whom we express our greatest concern. The secular community accords the church a position of respect. Privileges and favors are bestowed on church and clergy. Because the expectations in return are so reasonable and never resort to overt bribery or violence, we churchmen have learned to pacify any twinge of guilt or anxiety with the happy knowledge that the church is in a solid relationship with the wise and mighty of the world.

There are always a few, however, who have been nurtured by the Word, who kneel at the altar and hear the words "given and shed for the remission of your sins," who articulate the pain they feel over the distortions, adjustments, and denials that are the price a church must pay for public approval. They remind us in a most uncomfortable fashion of the prophets whom God has always sent to His people. We have learned how to handle them. We listen to them . . . and applaud. We invite them to address large gatherings. We lionize them. We acknowledge our appreciation of their fresh approach; someone had to say these things. At the same time we warn them that if they desire general acceptance, they must not be too radical. Most prophets can be handled by providing them an official office within the church. This makes for responsible churchmanship. And God must begin to shape another instrument.

Action

Finally the words of prophets must be put into action. As individual Christians and as churches we have had genuine difficulty in finding the best way to express compassion and to proclaim our Lord in judgment and grace. In the past many Protestant churches fell into the pattern of showing love and demanding justice through proclamation. Whenever an issue arose that demanded a moral judgment, a public proclamation was fashioned. This often eased the anxiety of a group of Christians. They were taking a stand; they were speaking for God. In most cases, however, the ultimate decision was made with little consideration being given to the statement. People tolerantly felt it was part of the job of the clergy and the church in general to act as watchdogs over the community's morality. When such proclamations moved into touchy areas or called for unpopular action, gentle admonitions were given over luncheon tables and in editorials, suggesting that the church stick to its important tasks of dealing with souls and spiritual matters and leave the matter of politics and the world in general to other people.

For the most part the underlying philosophy of public pronouncements was not adequately considered. Was the church hereby addressing its own members? Or was it speaking to the world? Was it clearly using its tools of Law and Gospel, or was it badly mixing the two in a desperate hope to accomplish something? Had it considered how the decision would be arrived at, or was it simply using a shotgun approach? Was the pronouncement cast in the general language of a theoretical statement of principle, or did it advocate a particular partisan view?

Some Christians began to distrust statements, saying the time for action had arrived. The period of the civil rights revolution in the United States provides a good illustration. Many young clergymen were distressed over the timidity of their leaders and embarrassed before the poor record of the American church during the preceding two centuries. Here was a clear denial of part of the very proclamation of the church. Many clergymen and lay Christians joined civil rights demonstrations. Some joined local organizations already in existence. Others created local associations of clergymen to fight their community's own problems of segregation and racial exploitation. Some accepted invitations from Christians in other parts of the country, notably the South, to stand with them in their fight for equality. Scores were arrested and jailed. Thousands joined marches and demonstrations, acknowledging their guilt for having done so little in the past and pledging specific help in the immediate future. Much of this was good. Genuine courage was shown before physical assault and the verbal vilification they met.

Unique Role of the Church

One's concern lies with the quality of leadership the church provided. Hindsight is always superior. In their desperation to overcome centuries of inactivity on the part of the churches, which had spoken benedictions upon the dominant community's exploitation, these men frequently became "rubber stamps" for other programs. In some cases men jumped on what was fast becoming a popular band-wagon. Even diehard segregationists saw the handwriting on the wall. In their complete identification with various actions of these other groups, however, they were in danger of losing their sense of the unique role of the church. The church could have played a prophetic role for each side in the controversy. For in the midst of the revolution there were excesses on both sides. Although basic justice was clearly on the side of the minority group, the civil rights movement became the arena in which many hoped to gain leadership and acclaim in given areas. Along with the responsible leadership that was exerted, many aggressive, irresponsible leaders arose and fanned the flames of hatred and violence. Where newly formed groups attempted to outbid others for popular support, they frequently wanted no reconciliation with the white community; demands were thrown down as gauntlets; charges of police brutality arose in situations where newsreel film indicated a scrupulous attempt on the part of the police to avoid racial friction. In these situations the church should have had the courage to speak to both sides. Some men honestly said that they feared to do so lest the minority community misunderstand and equate their action with that of white Christendom in the past. But courageous Christian leadership must extend even to the point of being misunderstood by friends and those to·whose welfare one is committed.

In general, however, we have erred on the side of too much caution and too little activity. We have so feared being misunderstood by people whose positions we valued that we remained in a state of strict neutrality. We defended this noncommital position by insisting that we were there to serve *all* people; we could not afford to alienate one segment of the population. Institutions, like people, can lose their souls while bent on preserving them. Churchmen have been hampered by an undue fear of conflict. Usually before

an issue has been clarified, they feel compelled to step into
a reconciling role of establishing peace.

Controversy

Many Christians are learning that controversy is a part
of life. In place of evading it or denying it, it is more helpful
to understand that it can be either destructive or creative.
Responsible controversy can be a sign of life and hope
within community and church. Some churches which had
fallen into a complacent rut of routine suddenly came alive
and were thrust back into a new dependence on God and
a more viable relationship with people because they were
stirred by a controversial issue.

Dan W. Dodson of the Center for Human Relations and
Community Studies at New York University has discussed
some of the fundamental propositions which underlie our
understanding of creative conflict. For him conflict and
controversy are the inevitable counterparts of freedom and
its resultant differences of opinion. "The church without
controversy is a conforming church." The people are either
so homogeneous or so withdrawn from the realities of the
world that they confront no new areas where agreement
has not already been achieved. When people care enough
about an area to fight for their view, we face commitment.
These differences must be brought out into the open and
examined in the light of the Word of God and the collective
judgment of the body of Christians.

From this point of view it is apparent that the church
should not desire the conformity that comes from fear to
express doubt about group beliefs. In too many churches
we find people meekly conforming to majority opinion. This
results in a general social fellowship of conformity that
avoids conflict, but it produces schizophrenic lives and cur-
tails witness. "The church cannot remain dynamic," Dodson
suggests, "without bringing the world to confrontation on

significant social issues." Make no mistake—the world will quickly cease her formal politeness and defense before the church when the church begins to touch the vested interests of various groups. When the church speaks God's law to the areas of race, business morality, war, and our increasing materialism, she can expect controversy both inside and outside her membership. Dodson's last principle is helpful to all who have wrestled with the method by which a church could assume a responsible position in its community: "It is illogical to expect that a congregation in the average modern church will endorse significant change through consensus." Because of varied interests and the position of influence which many church members hold in their communities, one cannot expect them to abdicate their former positions easily. A group moves through both consensus and conflict. Since one cannot achieve unanimity, and since the church nevertheless must act in the interim, the most that can be achieved in many cases is to make certain that Christians have confronted the full picture in the light of any direction offered by the Scriptures and the Confessions of the church.

Open Occupancy and Poverty

Consider a question that confronted many communities in the mid-sixties—open occupancy. It was apparent from notable defeats of such legislation (for example, in California) that the churches had to do more among their own members than have their clergyman sign a statement expressing his convictions. Laying aside the more brittle approach of an earlier day—public pronouncements—Christian groups sought for a more effective way of bearing witness. Notable was the approach of the Church Federation of Greater Indianapolis. They sent a memorandum to their member churches presenting facts and an interpretation, which an intelligent Christian would need in making a decision on this issue. They presented a factual overview of the ordinance and the experience of other communities which had such a law. They indicated the Christian opportunities in the light of the current situation in their city. Most striking was the section in which they stated in full the objections to open occupancy as raised by opponents to the bill, particularly the real estate board. They then detailed the position of those favoring the ordinance. A brief conclusion completed the 8-page memorandum. While no one questioned a man's Christian faith or his love if he opposed the bill, no one could oppose it without facing in some depth the multitude of points at which the faith spoke to this issue.

Or consider the policy developed in the United States for dealing with poverty. Because of the effect poverty has on people, the Christian finds himself concerned. He is not one who naively hopes to bring everyone to a golden middle-class standard, but neither can he rest easily while a sizable segment of the nation lives in conditions of ignorance, squalor, hunger, and illness. As we noted previously, however, we are not dealing with isolated phenomena. Nor are we dealing simply with certain families who "happen" to be poor. When one comes to know the family caught in the trap of poverty, he senses that everything seems to conspire to hold the parents and the children in this pit indefinitely. For the children growing up in such a family learn all the motivations and styles of life which reinforce the condition of poverty. Economic, social, and educational poverty are socialized at an early stage; children of welfare families learn early in life the patterns of thinking and acting that pretty well assure their continuation in a condition of dependency for another generation. So the vicious cycle continues generation after generation.

Robert Hess of the University of Chicago and others have demonstrated quite conclusively that the approach to poverty which our society still was taking in the mid-sixties was not designed to eliminate it, but to institutionalize a permanent "welfare class" in the nation. To illustrate his point, Hess suggests a fantasy wherein a group devises a fiendish plot to promote mental ill health among a segment of the population. The group of experts drawn together to devise a method for bringing about this result might recommend:

1. Maintain the family at a point of marginal subsistence;
2. Disrupt the family by assuring the absence of the father;
3. Treat attempts at self-help or economic improvement in a punitive fashion;
4. Frustrate the natural social and sexual desires of the mother;
5. Subject the families to suspicion and implicit accusation;
6. Deprive the family of self-direction and autonomy;
7. Create a public image of such families as dishonest, immoral, lazy, and illiterate; identify them by specific designations such as "welfare cases," "on relief," or with alphabetic designations such as "ADC."

It is apparent that the "fiendish plot" bears an uncomfortably close resemblance to current welfare policies. After several decades of this approach it should be clear that the situation has not improved but grown steadily worse. Welfare programs expanded; greater appropriations were made; large cities were spending over a million dollars a week on welfare, with the need still outdistancing the resources. The "war on poverty" launched by President Johnson opened even greater resources to be devoted to welfare families. Some observers expressed concern that programs might be restricted to dealing with consequences of poverty – illiteracy, dropouts, unemployment, delinquency, and crime – while the basic causes continued unimpeded.

80

More is needed than general programs designed to serve as preventive measures. Effective change, Hess argues, must be "directed at the early years, before the warping and crippling atmosphere of deprivation can permanently impair the physical, cognitive, and emotional faculties of the child and assign him an identity as a member of an inferior segment of our society."

Effecting Change

These illustrations are useful in showing the complexity of problems that will not yield to a sentimental or oversimplified solution. They also demonstrate areas in which the modern Christian must be concerned. Notice that effective action must be brought simultaneously on several fronts. Alteration in any area necessitates a fundamental change in thinking among people. People within the community — Christians in particular — must reexamine their basic attitudes toward many fundamental issues. This involves more than gaining new facts, for such attitudes are compounded of many fiercely held views. People are emotionally involved. Potential changes in some of these areas are likely to be threatening to them. Some are concerned that if the punitive quality is removed from welfare, pressures upon the entire society to work and advance will be undermined. Many are personally harsh in their judgments on the poor because they invest the situation with all the factors they have consciously squeezed from their own lives in their drive for success — lack of restraint, sexual freedom, lazy and undisciplined living, lack of responsibility. In dealing with others, they are unconsciously reinforcing their position, often with anxiety, for they fear the possibility of a personal fall into such a condition. Basic changes are needed in our thinking as individuals in crucial areas of modern urban living.

Institutional changes likewise are needed. Many agencies, we said, are complicating the situation in their very attempts to help. At times changes on this plane are easier to effect than on the first level. Here we are dealing with a small group — those who sit on the policy boards that control such welfare agencies. Again churchmen are involved. Their faith provides a vantage point for interpreting man and society which others lack. Agencies sponsored by the church could be in the vanguard of boldly experimenting with more imaginative programs of help. Instead of waiting for governmental groups to prod them to bring various procedures and facilities up to standards, agencies of the church could provide vision and light for groups that have difficulty in gaining support until a program proves workable.

Finally, however, decisions must be made in the public sphere. This may involve passing a law; it may involve the judgment of an important group, such as the real estate board in the question of open occupancy. This decision usually reflects the thinking of the community itself. Lawmakers remain more sensitive to what the mass of voters are saying than to what a few clergymen may be saying about ethical principles. Thus where, for example, churches have taken an active part in encouraging all of their people to sign a good-neighbor pledge — a statement that they would welcome into their community responsible persons of any race, religion, or national origin and work with them to maintain a desirable community for all — a decision on the part of a city council or a local board becomes easier. Such official groups tend to be rather conservative in reflecting the status quo; ordinarily they have great difficulty in moving too far ahead of their constituency. Even in the public domain, then, individual Christians and groupings of people of faith within congregations and larger organizations can become agents of necessary change.

When we illustrate specific areas where Christians need to exert their influence, we must remember that one task of the Christian is to keep his eyes lifted toward the future. He is therefore in a position to become aware of human need before others. In actual fact he has too often failed to fill this role. The church was not the first to call us to an awareness of the plight of Negroes during the forties or to the poverty-stricken in the sixties. Others stepped into the vacuum. Too frequently our institutional concerns prevented us from more faithfully filling our twin role of God's servants and His prophets in our age.

The Rev. John Wagner, an authority on the role of the church in urban culture, has placed a number of questions before Christians as they work together within congregations. He asks: Have congregations placed survival above mission? Will we free our pastors from administrative responsibilities to give more time to teaching? Will we give new forms of metropolitan church structures a strong position in the life of our congregations? Will Christians have the courage to risk entrance into fields of interest and concern which have been traditionally neglected by the church? Will our churches work redemptively in specific spots of community friction and alienation? Can we accept the appropriateness of having a small number of committed Christians meet community concerns with Christian conscience and action? Can we tighten church membership so that discipline and commitment become less esoteric? Will we initiate interdisciplinary dialog on major ethical issues of our society?

In this approach we destroy the wall that has separated the influence of faith from our world. "Social concerns" must cease being a separate category from "spiritual concerns." But in our work we recall Abbé Michonneau's warning that our task is not to try to patch up the ills of the world around us but to rebuild it completely. As militants filled with the Spirit of Christ, this becomes our order.

6

REBIRTH — RESTORED COMMUNITY

In the middle of the 1960s Otto Fuerbringer, managing editor of *Time* magazine, was asked to review all that the churches were experiencing, highlighting those actions which appeared most significant. He isolated five items as the most productive of change: First, the ecumenical dialog has shifted from the seminary to the level of the parish. Second, the claim of possessing special charismatic gifts has spread widely; churchmen in many bodies claim to have the Spirit's gift of speaking in tongues. The third trend focuses on the recovery of the inner city and a willingness on the part of the churches to experiment with new forms of the church there. Fourth, the impact of the church on social issues has grown tremendously in the early sixties. Fifth, a consolidation of theology is apparent.

Fuerbringer's observations speak to the heart of our concerns. Because of the prophetic call of such churchmen as Bonhoeffer and the fact that churches have found themselves catapulted into the midst of life at its most demanding points, Christians suddenly became aware of themselves standing in the marketplace with people who actively sought to know the Christian response to scores of controversial issues. Churches were faced with alternatives. To remain silent was to give comfort to those who fought to maintain a personal piety that did not relate to the crucible of the 20th-century marketplace. Failure to speak confirmed others in their impression that God had not spoken a meaningful word to our age and therefore placed sanctions upon a crass secularism.

A Christian Response?

The Christian, however, must think through his response to the urban world. We need more than random actions, uncorrelated and often conflicting reactions to new problems and challenges.

The logical beginning is to ask: Is there such a thing as a Christian response to the modern metropolis? There is a periodical with the subtitle *Man in Metropolis: A Christian Response*. The editors indicate that the most frequent criticism they receive is the question: "So you call that a Christian response?" Is there a Christian response that is different from a Jewish response — or that of an agnostic humanitarian? More specifically, is there a uniquely Christian response to the problems of water pollution or urban renewal?

Equally committed Christians will differ in their answers to these questions. We can, however, define the limits within which an answer must be given. The Christian senses his continuity with other modes of human life. As the handiwork of a common creator, he senses a root kinship with all who consciously or unconsciously affirm basic values of creation.

85

Thus there is a point where the Christian senses a keen kinship with a Jew or a humanitarian who is working for the fundamental rights of human beings in a given area of civil rights. Their motivations may differ; their methods of procedure may differ; their estimate of the ideal future may vary, but fundamentally they stand together as they share certain values regarding the worth of human beings who are superior to *things,* who are not to be degraded or manipulated – even for their own good. Within the last 10 years Christians have been rediscovering this common ground of understanding as they take more seriously their call to the world.

But there is another limit we must set that answers affirmatively: There *is* a Christian response! This is not to say that in any specific issue there is a single answer – *the* Christian response. Our day is filled with illustrations of two groups picketing for opposite solutions to a specific domestic or international issue – with churchmen in evidence in both groups. Few genuine issues are so simple and clear-cut that a single solution is beyond doubt the *only* Christian answer. But the Christian is in a position to give a unique and responsible answer. I use the term *responsible* as H. R. Niebuhr has defined it for a generation of Christians. This concept of the responsible action is most clearly seen in contrast to two classical answers. The first is the answer of Aristotle and all of the ethics which build on his foundation. Man is seen as a maker who constructs not only products but also aids in building the good man and the ideal society. To be human means to be in control of one's life. With reason and a will, a man is able to determine the future he desires and to work toward it. The ideals toward which men have striven are widely divergent, but the basic pattern of "man the maker" remains the same. The aim and end of life is the crucial question in this approach.

Another approach which has dominated scholarly and

popular thought begins with the concept of law. If the first uses a technical symbol, the second uses a political — man is a citizen under law. Man comes to self-awareness through confrontation with the law. In the case of the developing child, the aborigine, the scientist — that which permits him to know himself, to live, and to explore a discipline lies through the pathway of rules and laws. As in the former case, those who fall into this broad classification find a wide variety of focuses; but the beginning point of law is common.

Responsibility

It is in contrast to each of these approaches that we speak of the concept of responsibility. While the first two models have proved useful for generations of mankind, the new symbolism of responsibility is more faithful to the understanding of man. We have arrived at this symbolism on the basis of a developing theology and the social and psychological sciences. As a parallel to the earlier images, we would say the responsible man is the image of "man the answerer" — the man who is engaged in dialog, the man who is acting in response to action upon him. The biological and social sciences have taught us to picture man in a field of natural and social forces that are acting upon him and to which he is reacting. Man is constantly engaged in dialog with his world — he is reacting, answering, rejecting, adjusting, defending, and initiating in response.

On the practical level of life one does not usually act by consciously thinking of the ultimate ends of his actions and thereby determining his behavior. Nor is the abstracted question of mores, tradition, and law the key issue that determines action. The former two images become more useful when they are consciously interpreted in the context of response. Actually there are many passages in the earlier ethical writers that suggest an embryo awareness of this reality. But along with Niebuhr we suggest that, to ask how a Christian will respond to the urban world, we proceed best not by asking about ideals and hopes for the future nor about laws. "Yet the decision on which the future depends," Niebuhr summarized, "and whence the new law issues is a decision made in response to action upon the society, and this action is guided by interpretation of what is going on."

This is illustrated on the level of nation and individual. The new directions taken in the United States following the Civil War and during the administrations of Roosevelt and Kennedy obviously were responses to new situations—both internally and internationally. Specific decisions were not made through reference to the "good" or to "law." Also when a person suffers, he is affected and changed in character, not by the suffering itself but by how he reacts and responds to it. It is a dynamic process in which he is reacting to the total situation—which includes the ends he sees in life and his values and perceptions of how others are viewing him.

This view of responsible action involves, then, these ingredients: The response is made consciously, with awareness and intelligence. How we respond to anything is partially dependent on how we interpret it as part of a larger whole. America will interpret any specific action of Russia in terms of a greater attempt to understand the Russian mind, the philosophy of communism, and the broader movement of history today. Another element in responsibility is accountability—the anticipation of reaction to our response. As in a dialog, each statement or action looks both backward and forward. It is part of a whole. The final component is that of social solidarity—"it is a response to action upon us in a continuing discourse or interaction among beings forming a continuing society."

We have described this concept of "responsibility" at some length because it forms a useful key for interpreting the posture of a Christian in our complex world. We said it is more faithful to our modern mind-set. It is also more faithful to the Scriptures. Formerly we had difficulty in using much of the Bible when we asked primarily questions regarding the ends of life or about the laws of God. For too many people the concept of the ends degenerated into a vague idealism drawn from sections of the Bible — these became goals toward which the Christian was to strive. This approach is totally alien to the spirit of the Scriptures. In the second case corruption took place when God was pictured primarily as the great Lawgiver. When the prophets stood before the people of the Old Testament as they faced a crucial decision, to what did they point? It was not to some ideal goal, nor was it to the Law. They pointed to the God who was present in His action (perhaps through an enemy people) or in a deliverer whom He was to send.

The Responsible Christian

The Christian, then, is called into our modern urban setting to be a responsible man. He does not approach his task with the sentimentality of working with a future utopian model nor with the rigidity of applying set laws. He comes with the freedom of having been placed into a social and physical setting in which he is to respond. He comes to his task with sensitivity, consciously attempting to interpret that which he experiences. He is consciously a part of his social group; he responds knowing that he is accountable to his group and to God. This is the model of Christian responsibility; it finds continuity with other human responsibility. It becomes uniquely Christian as the man continues to ask what additional insight the Word is able to bring him. For him and other Christians within the church a prime motivation for any action lies in the fact that God has made known His will for people.

Thus he approaches any problem area of life not simply because it is a national disgrace, economically damaging, internationally dangerous, or socially destructive. He enters the problem area because God has spoken, and in this area people are being destroyed. They are being prevented from becoming that which God willed for them. Furthermore, he will not stand alone. Fellow Christians are formed and reformed by the same empowering Word. They too will begin to respond. Their interpretations may differ. They may relate the symptoms to different larger wholes. Therefore their solutions may suggest alternative courses of action. But as fellow Christians they will share their understanding of the problem and their suggested steps toward amelioration. Questions of priorities, strategies, results of alternative approaches — all will be discussed so that, where possible, concerted effort will result.

While Scripture does not provide specific judgments upon courses of action in a given problem area, it does provide us with an understanding of values which arise out of the story of God's action among His people. Thus many individual goals might be summarized in the simple phrase "restored community." God created us to be in fellowship with Him and in community with others. Sin destroyed both bonds. The rebellion of sin shows immediately in persons in whom guilt and anxiety have begun to fester, persons now driven to hide from God. It shows in their relationship to one another. Shame replaces their former pristine openness; charges, defenses, recrimination, pride, and murder now darken life in family and society. Community is broken.

Broken community has been the motif running through these pages. Fragmented people. Alienated individuals. Those crying for their share of life's treasures and those protecting their prior claim are symptoms of broken community. And the problem is of such dimensions that it will not yield to manipulation or techniques. The problem is deeper than ignorance or apathy. And the line between the 'good guys" and the "bad guys" cannot be easily drawn. The first guilty attempt at correction is to see all minority peoples, all poverty-ridden, all unemployed, all those jailed, as "good guys" — and those of the majority, respectable people living in unresponsive affluence, as evildoers. Those sensitive enough to be working for change become the "best guys."

The responsive Christian is freed from this illusion. The line of sin cannot be drawn between people; the line always runs through a man's life. Within the man who has not come to God — and this is more than saying that he is unchurched — the judgment of sin lies upon his whole life. This does not imply that he is vicious or immoral. He is, however, living for lesser gods who nevertheless demand a man's total commitment. Some live crassly for themselves. They consume others with no sense of remorse. Others may live for their children, for their job, for American democracy. One can bring such people into proximity. Laws and customs can demand respectable limits of conformity. But one does not achieve community. The Christian who consciously desires to right the wrongs of urban society is most conscious of the dilemma. He is aware of his own mixed motivations — his own enjoyment of privilege . . . his carefully protected image of "fearless spokesman" for the poor . . . his disgust when the outcasts don't respond . . . his practiced stance of humility. But mixed with these is an honest desire to be a faithful Christian . . . spontaneous service that does not measure the cost . . . a singing joy when one is helped.

The one whom God can use to work in this process of restoring community is the one who acknowledges the dilemma. He has himself been forgiven. He has been freed from false idealism and rigid legalism. Because he has faced the reality of sin, he is less prone to discouragement. And he sees the roots of sin still operative in his own life. Therefore he lives with a sense of continued dependence on God. He draws on God's own power in Word and sacraments.

He knows that evil and sin are not external to him. He knows that God still rules His world. So he works in faith, with the hope that God's will will eventually be carried out.

Here we come to the heart of our "theologizing" about life in megalopolis. For the Christian—and for the man who rejects Him—Jesus Christ is the Center. For in the events of His life, His death, and His resurrection a fundamental change has taken place. All of life is different because of it—even life that is heavily scarred by sin. Whether a man realizes it or not, God has bound him to every other man. John Harmon has reminded us that Jesus Christ has established peace among all men. This is a reality even while so much evidence seems to deny it. Christ is Lord *now!*

Therefore we are brothers. This awareness is the theological key for the life of the church in the city.

Six Steps Toward Action

How does this responsible action begin? We might consider six steps.

First, the process begins with repentance. We must face our selfishness, our evasions, institutional smugness, our fears, and our misunderstandings. These must be faced before God. In the light of our understanding of responsible action they must be interpreted as more than a failure to measure up to our own best selves. They are more than a breaking of Biblical laws. They are symptoms of our primary concern for ourselves—for our prestige, our possessions, and our comfort. They are symptoms of the tragic gap between our profession as Christians and our lives. To a great extent, changes have not occurred because we have not desired change. We have gone so far as to feel vaguely anxious about our failure to do something about people being broken in a slum. But we quickly discovered ways of discharging this feeling of guilt when it reached the point of discomfort. Those who work in social service agencies in the inner city tell a sad tale of middle-class suburbanites who come to do "volunteer" work. Too often they come out of a feeling of guilt or personal boredom. Thus when these personal needs are met by several sessions of "work," they become delinquent in continuing their service. Both the agency and the neighborhood people are worse off because of their abortive efforts.

Repentance is more than feelings of guilt or sorrow. True, repentance may begin here. But it moves on to include a change of mind, shifting one's life so that it begins to run in a new direction. The responsible Christian senses the need for becoming as sensitive to the needs of others as he has been to his own needs. The reality of this process might begin as he finds himself in the midst of troublesome situations. Responsible action finds its beginning in repentance before God.

Second, the Christian who would act responsibly must engage in a process of listening and learning. Complex urban problems will not yield to homemade solutions based on pet theories. Urban people have become hardened to stock formulations of the Gospel hawked at them by street-corner preachers, shouted by revivalists, and peddled in tracts by people at bus stops. A stance of humility and open-mindedness is necessary. This does not mean forsaking either the Gospel or courage. It does suggest a necessary pedagogical method.

We are describing a Christian who responds faithfully to a given situation. To interpret the situation correctly it is essential that he carry on more than a monolog with it. Dialog has become an overworked word in recent years. Yet it conveys a necessary insight. A Christian must enter into dialog with others in order to assess the true condition of the urban scene. This is the necessary first step toward effecting change.

Reuel Howe has suggested four marks of this "dialogical" person. He is, first, a total, authentic person. He is never one who uses a situation or other people for his own ends. He enters into the circumstances of life wholeheartedly, with heart as well as mind; he listens as well as speaks. Second, he is an open person. He is willing to reveal himself as well as have the sensitivity to receive the revelation of the other person. Further, the dialogical person is disciplined; this is to say, he is able to assume responsibility for himself and for others. He is able to accept the limitations as well as the opportunities which relationships offer. One's contribution must be made in the context of the contribution of others in the urban world. Finally, the dialogical person is a related person. Because he is able to respond to others, he can become responsible. He becomes one through whom God can work. As Howe says simply: "It is imperative, then, that a Christian be a dialogical person through whom the Word that gives life is spoken."

The third step the Christian must take is to realize that the arena of God's concern is much broader than any "religious" sphere. It seems shocking to the average Christian that there is a point at which he is opposed to "religion." We need to remind ourselves that nowhere do the Scriptures support "religion" as an unqualified good. Rather they are vociferous in their denunciation of any religion which enthrones idols in the place of God. The question forces itself therefore: Where are the areas in modern religious life that have created "idols" which have usurped the place of God — perhaps while retaining His name as a pious subterfuge?

There are two real worlds: the secular world and the world of faith. Each has its own values, goal, and styles of life. We fear that the religionist has created a third world — the world of religion. It is an artificial world where secularism thrives under the guise of symbols of the faith. It is not the world of faith; it is a form of this world that is destined to pass away. It is idolatrous, for it seeks men's loyalties.

It is deadly, for too many are unable to distinguish it from the true world of faith.

We must not equate this world of religion with the organized church. While "organization" and "institutionalization" have become dirty words with which to castigate the church in recent years, the problem is not this simple. The moment a group of Christians decide to do anything together, some form of organization becomes inevitable. This is not the problem. It is true that institutionalized churches become a chief source of that illegitimate world of religion. God eventually becomes the distant symbol behind real estate, buildings, programs, organizations, and projects that may have little bearing on the world or upon faith.

God's concern is about the world He made—a world fallen into sin, but a world which He loves and has redeemed. God calls men to faith in order to enter that world with His Word of life. He commissions His men to enter that world with service. They go bringing a word of judgment and of grace. They go hearing a voice different from that of the world; their lives of love are to attest to this.

As a fourth step a Christian (with fellow Christians) might analyze his congregation to determine at what points a change of policy and action is necessary in order to be of truest service to the urban world. The situation will vary with each church. Most churches, however, have fallen into patterns of thought and action in which routine has replaced conscious thought regarding the role of the congregation in its community and city. Patterns of life are perpetuated which are no longer effective. They were often designed for a group of people and a social setting that no longer exists. Forms of polity, role expectations of the ministry, methods of outreach, areas of church involvement in the community, and the corporate image the congregation unconsciously proclaims to its area may be badly suited for performing the mission of the church of faith. Between individual change in the Christian and desired change within the urban community lies change within the thought and structures of the local congregation.

Fifth, the Christian must live in conscious dependence on God's power as it is conveyed through the Word. Luther once spoke of the church as the people of God united in the Word of God. The Word is not restricted in some static or fundamentalistic sense to the Bible. It is the total Word of God—preeminently the incarnate Word in Jesus Christ; the written Word of the prophets, evangelists, and apostles; the visible Word conveyed through the sacramental water, bread, and wine; the living Word as it is spoken by men today. This Word initially imparts life to men; it continues to mold and shape their lives—their thinking and their acting.

Thus while the Christian must live much of his life of "faith active in love" out in the world, he must continue to withdraw in order to refuel himself with the Word. We described the necessary rhythm of assembly and dispersion. In the assembled state Christians are strengthened for their task in the world. Enthusiasm for service must never endanger a man's spiritual life by sanctioning his separation from his source of life in God's Word.

The sixth step, action, follows. In moving out into new frontiers, problems are often clearer than solutions. Therefore many of our actions will be tentative and experimental. But a beginning will be made. There is a danger that the problems loom so large that they appear insoluble and as a result paralyze us into a helpless state of doing nothing. Flexibility will remain important. Christians who are making significant contributions to urban America today have tried many approaches. When one leads to a dead end, they simply drop that approach or modify it. But they continue to act.

Action will lie on several fronts. Much of the service needed remains that of the individual. An individual responds to a neighboring family when the mother is hospitalized and basic help is needed for the children. A Christian volunteers in answer to a request for help in an inner-city literacy program; he sits down with one person to teach him to read and write. A high schooler devotes two weeks during a summer vacation to serve as teacher in a church vacation Bible school program. An individual takes the initiative to gather togethr a group of his neighbors to clean up the alley behind their property and begin a program of rat eradication.

In a natural way these individual actions flow into group actions. Someone organizes the program of literacy so that not only one person is taught to read, but scores of adults. As more people are involved—or as more resources are needed to attack the problem properly—higher levels of organization are needed. In larger programs a staff must be employed to direct, coordinate, and train volunteer efforts. To be heard on the upper levels of city government, many will have to join together to represent a large enough number of voters so that politicians will take the request seriously.

This process in turn has naturally flowed into the next higher level of organization. When one meets problems which affect the region and the nation, the voices and actions of thousands need to be correlated in order to be heard by a state or federal government. The problem of race demanded an answer on a level beyond that of the unprejudiced individual. It demanded more than local ordinances enforcing open occupancy. It finally needed federal laws which dealt with the nationwide aspects of discrimination and segregation.

Our goal is restored community. The test we can apply to any proposed action is: Will this lead to healing and restored community? We will work on many fronts; we will work on many levels. We will be allied with many groups; our enemies will appear in many guises. A rebirth is taking place within Christendom . . . and within the metropolis.

Our Lord has sent us to a world that is different from any we have known before. But it remains His world. Therefore we are to be there. We are to work with hope. For we are the people through whom the Lord would reign in His world of the city.

QUESTIONS FOR DISCUSSION

1. In your community what are the most significant evidences of a movement toward greater urbanization? How have these factors influenced you and those closest to you?

2. In what ways has your church addressed itself to some of the problems and challenges of a growing metropolitan culture? Are there specific areas of need in which it could provide aid?

3. How can the church become involved in community issues without becoming partisan?

4. Read the Book of Acts, noting the sensitive spirit of concern for people evidenced there.

5. How do you react to the heavy criticism leveled against churches in recent years? To what extent is it justified? exaggerated?

6. Consider a specific issue (such as the Civil Rights movement) or a local issue (such as the building of a hospital) and ask what type of influence Christians had either individually or collectively as a church in bringing about a favorable result.

7. Do you agree with the judgment that the church has not been as conscious of ministering to the public sphere as it has to the private?

8. In what ways are the various churches in your city working together on bigger problems that demand more than the attention of a single congregation?

9. Find illustrations of churches working in various types of urban situations — slums, high-rise apartments, new suburbs, integrating communities, luxury apartments, etc. — where a creative and effective task apparently is being performed.

10. American folklore has associated piety and the rich life with the countryside, and sin and corruption with

the "big city." Analyze your reaction to this view-point. Do you agree? Why? Is change taking place?

11. How might Protestant churches maintain patterns of congregational freedom and yet achieve the strength that comes from a unified strategy?

12. Chapter IV describes renewal within parishes, among parishes, and outside of parishes. Explore the sig-significance of such renewal for your community.

13. The judgment was expressed that Christians often are unduly afraid of controversy and conflict and thus seek premature reconciliation. Reflect upon any recent occasion in church or community where a better understanding of the function and process of conflict would have been helpful.

14. On the basis of Chapter VI, how would you describe a socially responsible Christian?

15. Summarize the unique role of the church in the creation of an urbanized culture.

FOR FURTHER READING

Campbell, Will D. *Race and the Renewal of the Church.* Philadelphia: Westminster Press, 1962.

Stringfellow, William. *A Private and Public Faith.* Grand Rapids, Mich.: Eerdmans, 1962.

Webber, George W. *God's Colony, in Man's World.* New York: Abingdon Press, 1960.

Winter, Gibson. *The Suburban Captivity of the Church.* New York: Doubleday & Co., Inc., 1961.

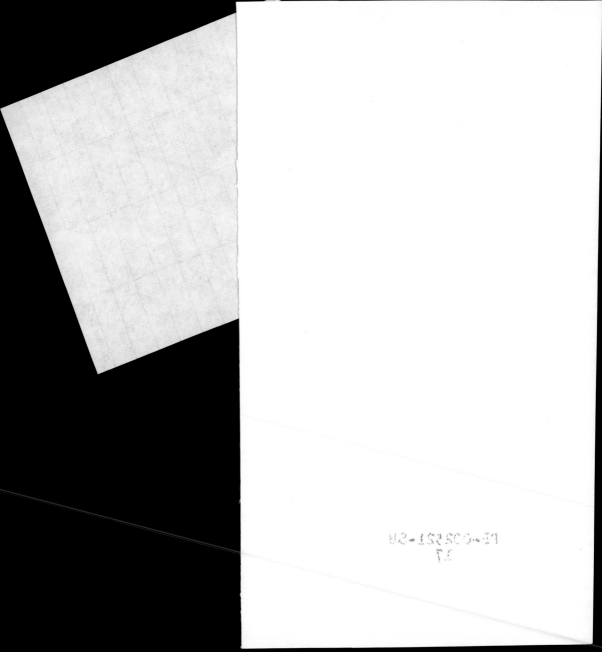

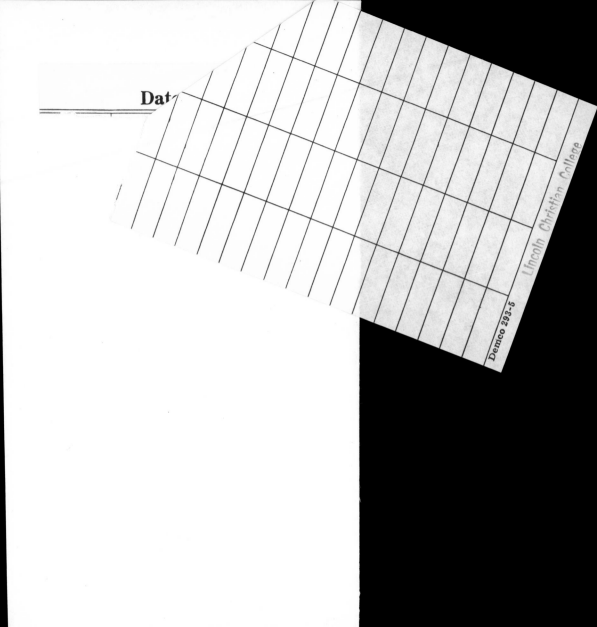

Dat

Date Due